THE DOGWATCH

Also by Ted Jones

LEARN TO SAIL

THE SAILBOAT CLASSES OF NORTH AMERICA

THE OFFSHORE RACER

THE SMALL BOAT SAILOR'S BIBLE

RACING FOR THE AMERICA'S CUP 1974

CHALLENGE '77: *Newport and the America's Cup*

THE
Dogwatch

By Ted Jones

W · W · Norton & Company

New York · London

*Dedicated to Humphrey B. Simson
who is directly responsible for
about 10,000 miles of these yarns*

Copyright © 1981 by Theodore A. Jones
Published simultaneously in Canada by George J. McLeod
Limited, Toronto. Printed in the United States of America.
All Rights Reserved
First Edition

Library of Congress Cataloging in Publication Data

Jones, Theodore A
  The dogwatch.

  Includes articles which originally appeared in One-
design & offshore yachtsman and boating magazines.
  1. Yachts and yachting—Addresses, essays, lectures.
2. Sailing—Addresses, essays, lectures.
GV813.J63   1981   797.1   79-27681
ISBN 0-393-03252-3

1 2 3 4 5 6 7 8 9 0

Contents

Introduction 7

Chapter I *Heritage*'s Race to the Races 13

II *Aground Under the Triborough Bridge* 28

III *A Cruise Down the Inland Waterway* 38

IV *Record Passage* 59

V *Record Passage In Reverse* 73

VI *The Bermuda Races* 81

VII *Sailing Transatlantic* 126

VIII *Many, Many Yachts* 152

IX *There Are No Cows at Block Island* 162

X *Zap!* and the Fogbound Baron 178

XI *Saint Petersburg to Fort Lauderdale* 188

XII *How It All Started* 217

INTRODUCTION

Ted Jones Takes the Dogwatch

I HAD BEEN WITH *One-Design & Offshore Yachtsman* magazine about a year when Bruce Kirby, the editor, asked me of I would like to do a regular column. I was naturally anxious to do it in spite of his warning that it would have to be a regular thing and that sometimes it was difficult to keep grinding out words that people would want to read every month. The first column appeared in December 1966. Some columns and articles were easy to write and some months there was a lot of balled up yellow paper in the waste basket. Others will have to judge whether or not they were all readable or carried a worthwhile message.

Bruce said I could have the back page—that it was probably the best location in the magazine—and asked that I think about a title that would give it some continuity. We ended up calling it "Ted Jones Takes the Dogwatch," which was the title it carried for many years. "The Dogwatch" is a double-entendre combining the jargons of both sailing and journalism. I have never been a journalist in the proper sense; rather, I have always considered myself someone with a pervasive interest in sailing who has had the good fortune to be able to write about his favorite subject and get paid to do it. So, the inference that I am one of the newsroom staffers taking the dogwatch to wait for late news developments after the regular edition has gone to press (which is the journalistic meaning of the term) is a bit fraudulent. The dogwatch to an offshore sailer is that period late in the afternoon (not midnight to 0400 as some mistakenly believe) when the four-hour watch is "dogged" or split in two, allowing the watches to rotate to the other time periods for the next twenty-four hours. I guess I have stood enough of these to make this use of the term legitimate.

The sailor's dogwatch is the only time during the day when both watches have an opportunity to socialize. In the old days—and sometimes even today—it was the time when a shot of grog was passed out to all hands and sea stories would be swapped.

Over the years, a fair number of sea stories were printed in the pages of *O-D&OY—Yacht Racing—Yacht Racing/Cruising* (as the magazine has variously been called) under my byline, and I have included in this collection the ones that seem now to be the most interesting.

Then there were a lot of events that I witnessed or participated in as a magazine editor or contributor that, usually because of limitations of space, never made it into print. The more memorable of these have been included here, recorded for the first time.

Until very recently, the magazine was devoted exclusively to the subject of yacht racing. Except for an occasional article in other magazines, I have been denied an outlet for what have been some of the most interesting experiences either cruising or just "banging around" in sailboats (there's one powerboat story—Chapter X). Here, I thought, was an opportunity to set down some of the more interesting, most instructive, and/or funniest of these.

In some cases words written for a periodical do not stand up under the pressure of time, like the month I explained how, with a little common sense it was not too hard to navigate around Block Island, and that very month got lost in the fog there (Chapter IX). Sometimes they are changed by subsequent events. In these cases the

Introduction

9

tale has been wrapped up as much as possible.

Acknowledgment is given to those magazines which first published some of the stories found here. I am particularly grateful to Knowles L. Pittman, *O-D&OY*'s founder, first editor, and publisher for providing the original forum for these tales, and to his successor *Yacht Racing/Cruising* publisher, George A. Eddy, for the same thing and for being a shipmate in some of them. Thanks also to all the other shipmates, skippers, and crews, who participated in the events chronicled here and helped make them tellable tales.

TED JONES

Newport, Rhode Island

THE DOGWATCH

I

Heritage's Race to the Races

ON SATURDAY, MAY 30, 1970, Charlie Morgan's 12-Meter *Heritage* left Saint Petersburg, Florida, bound for Stamford, Connecticut and the June America's Cup trials. It had been a race of sorts—a race against time. *Heritage* had been delayed by a series of misfortunes: an accident at her launching, injury to her owner, and finally an unusually early tropical storm.

Heritage, under command of offshore racer Peter Bowker, made good time to Fort Lauderdale—where some of the bugs were ironed out of her seagoing hatches and temporary living quarters. Then, in company with her tender *Alert* under the command of John Bolton, *Heritage* shoved off nonstop for Stamford, about one thousand miles to the NNE.

With Bowker, who was cook and navigator in addition to skipper, were Fred Bickley, an air force lieutenant on temporary duty with *Heritage* for the summer; Rory Burke, a rigger from Stamford, Connecticut and one of *Heritage*'s winch grinders; Tom Dudinsky from Saint Petersburg—also a winch grinder; Jim Guard from Riverside, Connecticut, *Heritage*'s "bosun"; and the author, who kept a tape-recorded log of the trip—excerpts of which follow.

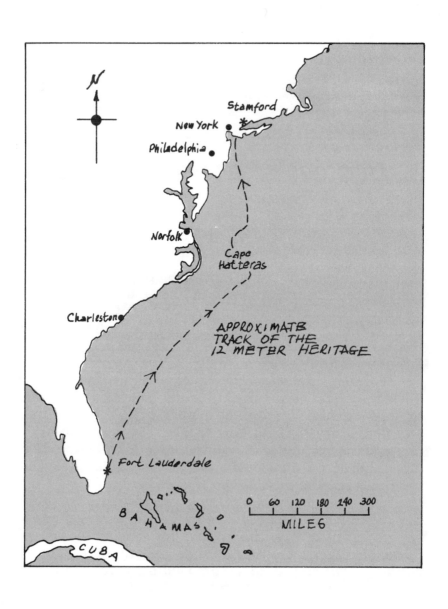

Heritage's Race to the Races

It's Wednesday, June 3. At ten minutes to nine we left the dock—under the bridge and out through the breakwater at 2105. Course is twenty-five degrees—7 1/2 knots at least—more like 8 knots. We have *Panacea*'s mainsail up and a storm jib. Peter just set watches, and we are on our way.

We have left Lauderdale astern. The weather is beautiful. The wind is blowing east with a little bit of south in it at fifteen knots, and we are making nine knots through the water.

Peter Bowker is in command, and Peter and I are on deck at the moment. I will go off at midnight, and I won't be back until 0800. We have four-on, four-off, four-on, eight-off watch system with two on deck at a time with Peter navigating and cooking not standing watches.

It's 0950 Thursday, June 4, and our D.R. puts us about fifty miles abeam of Cape Kennedy. This boat has *some* motion. She really bounces over these Gulf Stream seas. We have to crawl on the foredeck on our hands and knees, and every time you come on deck you have to be very careful of your footing. We are even wearing safety harnesses in the daytime, and we hook them to the wires that are strung from the forward end of the cockpit all the way to the stemhead.

It's now 1645 on Thursday, June 4, and I am sitting at the wheel of *Heritage*. Still have chute up—from Homer Dennius's sixty-footer *Rage*—and small main and the storm jib, and we are sailing along at about 9 knots. We spurt up to about 11 1/4 knots with just about every wave. A little while ago I was sitting on the bow, and the sensation of speed was tremendous. She has great power even with this reduced rig. She just shoots along.

Boy, is it hot below. "What's the temperature below Tom?"

"About eighty-five or ninety, I guess."

And very wet, very humid down there—very sticky—nice on deck though. Just two little hatches. We have one companionway of sorts and another little plastic hatch in the tailer's hatch, and it gets pretty stifling down there. Peter was finally able to raise our towboat the *Alert* at 1300. They were just a little bit north of the Cape (Canaveral) when we were abeam of it, heading for Charleston to refuel. We hope to be able to pick her up tomorrow morning. We shall see. The way we're going now, we don't need her.

"What do you think, Tom?"

"I think it's great!"

It's a little after four in the morning on Friday, June 5. I think. I said "I think" because I'm reminded of Peter Bowker's story of the time he and another fellow took a Bermuda 40 north to Moorehead City. When they got in his companion said, "I'll go up to the store and get some ice." Peter said, "You can't go to the store today —it's Sunday." His companion said, "It is not, it's Saturday." So, they finally asked the dockmaster what day it was. He said, "It's Monday."

Anyway, we are charging along following the Gulf Stream north.

Heritage boils along in the Gulf Stream shortly after her departure from Fort Lauderdale. Hatches were covered temporarily with plywood, leaving only two small openings for egress, exit, and ventilation. Note absense of lifelines. Two lines running diagonally to the bow were rigged for hooking on with safety harnesses.

Heritage's Race to the Races

17

It is 1830 on Friday, June 5. Fred Bickley has just discovered that the pin and chainplate assembly on the starboard side has backed halfway out. We are going to tack and try to get it back in.

The time is now 2020 on Friday, June 5. We jibed onto the other tack to fix the chainplate, and while we were working on that we discovered a slight rip in the mainsail so we took the main down. We got squared away on the other tack. Now we find that there's a crack in the chainplate assembly, and we're contemplating what to do about it. Possibly go into Moorehead City.

It is 0130 on Saturday, June 6. The wind is from the SSW, and it is really brisk, really brisk. We are having typical Gulf Stream weather. Big black clouds going over. On one side of the cloud, very little wind, and on the other side of the cloud there will be a lot of wind. I have no idea how hard it's blowing. It's very dark, and it's very difficult to tell. We are really ripping off the knots.

We decided to carry on with the chainplate pin the way it was. We managed to get a cotter pin in to hold the clevis pin in position, and the cracks in the weld don't appear to be in a critical spot. The alternative of going into Moorehead City seemed to be unnecessary as it wouldn't accomplish very much. We are a little bit further offshore than Peter figured we should be, so we have been trying to correct and change our course back to about 030 degrees but have not had too much success holding it. After a while, if it keeps up like this, we'll probably jibe.

Heritage boils along in the Gulf Stream shortly after her departure from Fort Lauderdale. Hatches were covered temporarily with plywood, leaving only two small openings for egress, exit, and ventilation. Note absense of lifelines. Two lines running diagonally to the bow were rigged for hooking on with safety harnesses.

Heritage's Race to the Races

It is 1830 on Friday, June 5. Fred Bickley has just discovered that the pin and chainplate assembly on the starboard side has backed halfway out. We are going to tack and try to get it back in.

The time is now 2020 on Friday, June 5. We jibed onto the other tack to fix the chainplate, and while we were working on that we discovered a slight rip in the mainsail so we took the main down. We got squared away on the other tack. Now we find that there's a crack in the chainplate assembly, and we're contemplating what to do about it. Possibly go into Moorehead City.

It is 0130 on Saturday, June 6. The wind is from the SSW, and it is really brisk, really brisk. We are having typical Gulf Stream weather. Big black clouds going over. On one side of the cloud, very little wind, and on the other side of the cloud there will be a lot of wind. I have no idea how hard it's blowing. It's very dark, and it's very difficult to tell. We are really ripping off the knots.

We decided to carry on with the chainplate pin the way it was. We managed to get a cotter pin in to hold the clevis pin in position, and the cracks in the weld don't appear to be in a critical spot. The alternative of going into Moorehead City seemed to be unnecessary as it wouldn't accomplish very much. We are a little bit further offshore than Peter figured we should be, so we have been trying to correct and change our course back to about 030 degrees but have not had too much success holding it. After a while, if it keeps up like this, we'll probably jibe.

Heritage's Race to the Races

We're approaching Cape Hatteras. We should be there some time early this morning.

We had a little excitement at four this morning. It had been raining on the eight-to-twelve watch and again from midnight to four, and Peter decided that we had better change our heading. Wind was then out of the south: We changed our heading to pass Hatteras to about 030 degrees, but we couldn't hold that so we decided that we'd hold onto what we could which was about 040 degrees or 050 degrees, sometimes 060 degrees until the change of the watch at four at which time we jibed with some small difficulty. Right in the middle of the jibe Peter had started to get the main in. I was on the helm with the last of the thunderstorm going through. It turned out we had a frontal passage, and the wind went from south to west like "zap," and of course the boom swung over and fetched up on the backstay. Fortunately, the main was in enough so that no damage was done. We jibed back and got squared away and made a proper jibe some ten minutes later.

Everything is water aboard *Heritage.* We have water coming up from the bottom, we have water coming down from the top, and we have water coming across from the sides. Everything is soaking wet and rather unpleasant, but it's warm and sunny out on deck today, and you don't even mind when the spray comes aboard.

Below, things are pretty much of a shambles. It's awfully stuffy down there. I imagine as the day wears on it's going to get hotter below and it will be difficult to sleep.

We're going to talk to the *Alert* in a little while to try and rendezvous as we approach the Jersey Shore.

Heritage's Race to the Races

1000 Saturday, June 6.

PETER: *"Alert,* this is *Heritage,* over."

JOHN: "Go ahead *Heritage,* this is *Alert."*

PETER: "John, I'm about twenty-five miles ESE of Diamond Shoal, over."

JOHN: "We'll be off Wilmington just about twelve, another two hours. What was your position comeback?"

PETER: *"Heritage* back to *Alert.* Our position—twenty-five, two five, miles ESE Diamond Shoal. Twenty-five miles ESE Diamond Shoal. Do you read that, over."

JOHN: "I find it a little hard to estimate when you are going to make New York, but what do you say at this point?"

PETER: "Sometime on Monday, John. Sometime on Monday, over."

JOHN: "The *Alert.* What's the weather like up there where you're at?"

PETER: "It's pretty nice here today The sun is shining. We got rid of all that rain and squalls we had yesterday. It's blowing about eighteen from the SW. If there is nothing further John, I'll talk to you at 1300, same channel. *Heritage* clear.

1215 Saturday, June 6. That sizzling noise (on the tape) is fresh Dolphin frying in the pan which we have, courtesy of Tom Dudinsky. Caught it about—oh, just in time for lunch, about quarter to twelve. It's about quarter after twelve, and we're going to have fresh Dolphin cooked by Mr. Bowker. [It was the tastiest fish I'd ever eaten.]

Heritage's Race to the Races

1430 Saturday, June 6. Wind has lightened, and the seas are calm, and we've got the *Rage* chute up again. Going along very nicely. Slipping along very, very smoothly—seven knots—eight knots. We had to make a few adjustments to the pole. The end was broken off for some reason. We don't know exactly how that happened, but Freddy discovered it yesterday. We put a couple of hose clamps around it, and now we're back in business again.

It's 2115 on Saturday, June 6, and we are past Hatteras by about 60 miles, and we have about 180 miles to go to Cape May. We have talked to John, and he is trying to get around Hatteras in a bad rainstorm, and we can see it now; there's a squall coming up on us. We're still running under the chute. We're probably going to take it down in a few minutes. The forecast is for northwest winds which should blow us nicely right into New York harbor tomorrow or a little bit later than tomorrow; maybe tomorrow night or early Monday morning. But first we'd better get the chute down.

It's 2320 on Saturday, June 6. The wind has gone very, very light. The thunderstorms that were all around are still all around, but nothing's materialized; great lightning displays, almost no wind and no rain as yet.

So here we are at 0445 on Sunday morning, and we haven't progressed very far. Going back to the eight-to-midnight watch. We had a frustrating night toward the end. At the change of the watch we took the spinnaker down and put the jib up. We were going along in a northeaster and that quit; that midnight-to-four watch must have been the most frustrating watch of the whole trip. Around, around in circles in light air, and then it would pour down rain. I was not on deck. I was in my bunk when it was going on, having bad dreams about various things; waking up and realizing where I was and wishing I were somewhere else. Right now we have a north wind which is rather unusual. We have the small jib and the *Panacea* mainsail up, and it's really not enough sail to drive the boat, and she short of pays off and reaches for a while and then she'll luff, shudder, and when you curse a little and try to get her back she pays off and reaches again. It is not very satisfying sailing. We might wait till they change the watch again, and we'll get enough bodies on deck to put the big genoa up and maybe get some drive out of her. Of course, by that time the whole thing may change again, who knows?

It's 1130 Sunday morning, June 7. We spent a lonely few hours doing very little. On the four-hour watch this morning from four to eight we were roughly headed for France, I think, making about twenty miles in the four hours. We're now off the entrance to Chesapeake Bay. Let's see, looking at the charts it's a little better than sixty miles, so our ETA of sometime Sunday is very optimistic. Sometime Monday is even optimistic at this point because John has preceded us into Cape May and will have to wait for us. We don't have much wind now. It's out of the NNE, and we're proceeding on the starboard tack with the genoa set in eight knots of breeze. Very light; very pleasant; nice sunshine.

It's 1300 on Sunday, June 7, and we have gone back on the port tack; genoa set; and we're making about a thirty-degree heading.

Peter has just prepared a delicious luncheon of chili and salad. I'm drinking the last cold beer.

Heritage's Race to the Races

My watch says that it is 0215 and it's Monday and it must be the eighth of June. We're not going to make it by Sunday. We spent all afternoon, Sunday, slamming and banging and making almost no progress at all. The light northwest wind we had went around to the west and pretty well quit, so we spent the afternoon sitting with the genoa just barely full and making two knots.

We got the Norfolk marine operator this afternoon and talked to Laura Morgan. She said that Charlie's in Westchester for the June trials which started today. We talked to John, which we didn't think we would be able to do. He's going to spend the night in Cape May, and we're going to talk to him at 0800 this morning. At that time we should be close enough to Cape May so that he can come out and find us and pick us up. It looks as if we're not going to get any wind to speak of, and we'd make better time under a tow, particularly if the sea stays smooth. But right now we have a nice northwest-by-north breeze, something in that order, and we have finally a 12-meter chute set, a 3/4-ounce spinnaker which is lovely and big, and blue and orange and white, and we're making about six knots. All is well at this point . . . we would like to get there.

It's just a little after four on Monday morning, and we've just had a delightful watch. Twelve to four with the spinnaker up; the wind came in and I guess we are probably cutting along at eight knots.

It was a little after two when we gave John some bearings from Delaware lightship to pick us up, and we now have him in sight. He is coming over our quarter

Heritage's Race to the Races

just as pretty as can be. When word came that John was coming on board, the offwatch came on deck.

John put *Alert*'s pulpit over our stern, and all the crew except Peter hopped off on the *Alert*. John and his boys hopped aboard *Heritage*.

So now everybody's been aboard the *Alert* who was aboard *Heritage* except Peter, and everybody who's been aboard *Heritage* except Peter has been aboard the *Alert*. The boys have all had showers.

"We bathed; clean bod!"

And now it's ten after midnight on Tuesday, the something or other of June. I have to look at my watch to tell what day it is. We dropped sail about sundown as the breeze was dying, and we're now under tow and have been under tow since about eight o'clock approaching Barnegat lightship. We are estimating Sandy Hook at 0500 and Verrazano-Narrows Bridge at 0600. The Brooklyn Bridge at 0700 and Stamford, Connecticut at 1100. I talked to Peter Watson in the office this morning, through the Norfolk marine operator, and they do know that we're expected at the first light in New York harbor. So maybe we'll have a reception in the morning. We have received orders from Charlie (through John Bolton on the *Alert*) that as soon as we pass Sandy Hook out comes the temporary cockpit, off come the hatches and we get *Heritage* in racing trim.

It's 0600, Tuesday morning, and we have been under tow since 2000 last night. We're just now turning Sandy Hook. Our ETA slipped about an hour all the way through so it looks like we'll be in Stamford at

Heritage's Race to the Races

noon or something like that. So we've been towing at 9 1/2 to 10 knots. Rory and Tom are on deck and are very anxious for everyone to get out of the rack so we can start taking things apart. We took the tape off the hatches and we're about to see the great unveiling.

It's 1030, Tuesday, and I'm aboard the *Alert.* We've just successfully negotiated the East River, and we're about to pass City Island. Stepping Stone's Light is to starboard. We're on our way into Stamford. We'll be in Stamford in an hour and a half. *Heritage* is getting all cleaned up. You wouldn't recognize her from the boat that we've been sailing out in mid-ocean.

We spotted a blue sloop on a collision course, just off Matinecock Point and it turned out to be Tom Young's *Shearwater* with Charlie waving his arms frantically on the foredeck. They came alongside and Charlie stepped aboard *Alert* and drove us into the middle of the spectator fleet near "32 A" watching *Valiant* and *Intrepid.*

Tomorrow *Heritage* joins them.

It turned out to be a tough summer for *Heritage,* her skipper, and her crew. Not surprisingly, considering our late arrival at the June trials, *Heritage* was not competitive with the other Twelves. Nor did she improve in July when the America's Cup contenders met again. The boat was not fast, her tactics were not remarkable, and her crew work was not smooth. Charlie was acting as his own design consultant, his own coach, his own financier, and trying to be skipper of the boat too. Charlie tried to do too much himself, was the common thread of dock scuttlebutt.

Radical changes to *Heritage*'s rig improved her con-

Shortly after their rendezvous off Cape May, New Jersey, the crews of *Heritage* and *Alert* trade places, leaving Peter Bowker alone aboard *Heritage*—spinnaker set.

siderably, but in August she was only just about as good as the other new Twelve, *Valiant,* which had not been as fast as *Intrepid.* Early in the August trials, I had watched *Heritage* for two-thirds of a race wage a close but losing fight against *Valiant,* and when the outcome was no longer in doubt I headed my photoboat, *ZAP!,* to the course where the French and Australians were racing to see who would be the America's Cup challenger.

"ZAP!, This is *Alert,* over," my radio crackled to life about an hour later. It was John Bolton aboard the *Heritage* tender, and I responded.

John's voice sounded close to tears as he said into the radio, "Ted, we're at the dock now and the Committee's launch (New York Yacht Club's Selection Committee) is headed our way. Looks like we've had it—I'll call you back later."

A few minutes later he called again to say that the Committee had thanked Charlie and *Heritage*'s crew for their efforts but that they were no longer needed in the America's Cup trials.

II

Aground Under the Triborough Bridge

FOLLOWING THE TRANSATLANtic Race to Denmark, Humphrey Simson's *Kittiwake* was shipped home to New York. The freighter, on which she was deck cargo, docked in Brooklyn on the East River, and Barney Compton and I, who had been watch captains on the race, were with Humphrey to help get *Kittiwake* offloaded, cleared through customs, and motor her—with masts on deck—to Minneford's Yacht Yard in City Island. The routines of taking delivery of a 47-foot, 30,000-pound sailboat from shipside can make a tale in themselves, but having made about twenty of these deliveries, it was old hat to me. I appointed myself "cruise director" and tried to show Barney and Hump how it was done.

We had hoped to be away by ten o'clock to catch the current, but the paperwork took most of the morning, and while Humphrey chased around looking for the "checker," the Customs inspector, and other officious officials, Barney and I kept *Kittiwake* from grinding her aluminum hull against the steel hull of the freighter from which she had been launched at the crack of dawn. Hopelessly late, we finally got away about one o'clock just as the current turned against us.

The stage of the tide is critical in making any passage through New York harbor. The current runs swiftly everywhere, and in Hell Gate—the narrow channel be-

Aground Under the Triborough Bridge

tween the Bronx and Queens—it runs as swiftly as 4 1/2 knots. In a boat that does 7 1/2 knots (under power) you find you're either doing 12 knots or 3. Only for very brief periods is there slack water.

Since the spars were on deck we were able to get under the liftbridge which crosses the east passage behind Welfare (Blackwells—now Roosevelt) Island. This saved us a bit of time, because the current is about half-a-knot less there than in the main channel on the Manhattan side. But swinging around Hallets Point past the Pearl Wick Hamper factory into Hell Gate, the current met us head on, full force. As the river passes under the Triborough and Hell Gate bridges, it makes a sweeping bend to the west and then joins the Harlem River at a right angle. The depth varies from thirty-five to one hundred feet. Naturally, in this typography, the water churns in deep rips, and the velocity of the current is much less on the downstream, inside of the bends.

Still playing tour guide, I explained to Humphrey and Barney that I planned to steer *Kittiwake* diagonally across the current to the Bronx side where there should be as much as two knots less current along the Wards Island shore. I was so positive that neither questioned my decision. I had the fleeting thought that we should check the chart, but hell, there's plenty of water right up to the banks on either side. I remembered that from my many previous trips.

I headed for a spot on the shore under the north tower of the bridge where there was a small beacon. Behind us was a spindle on a pile of rip-rap about one hundred yards off the shore. Surely if I stayed outside of the line between those two markers we would be okay.

Boom! *Kittiwake* hit hard, and before I could spin the wheel to head her out toward deep water the current grabbed her bow and spun us the other way. In a split second we were hard aground with no way to get ourselves turned around. *Kittiwake* heeled over as the force

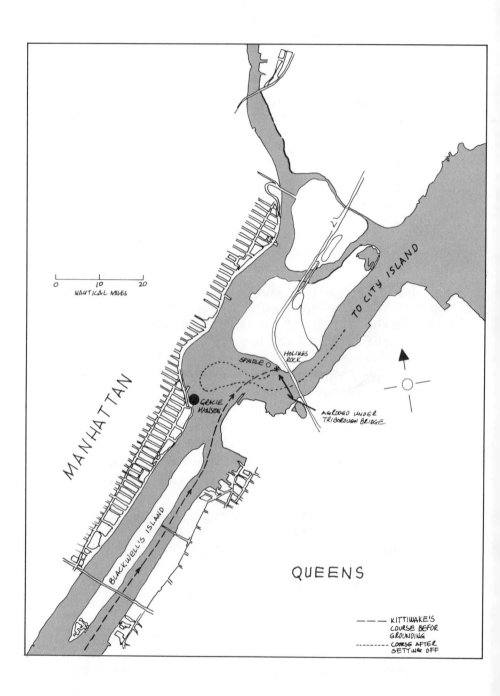

Aground Under the Triborough Bridge

of the current swept broadside around her hull, and she bobbed fretfully in the turbulence, her keel grinding on what in those swift currents could only be solid rock.

A quick look around showed us that we had caught the edge of a rock ledge which extends out into the river just to the line between the spindle and the beacon. (The East River chart shows two and three feet there at low water with "Holmes Rock" awash.) Along the rest of the river you would scrape your topsides on the bulkhead before your keel touched, but I had found one of the few exceptions. We were in no immediate danger, but we had grounded on a falling tide and would be there for the rest of the day unless someone pulled us off soon.

I was into my third apology to Humphrey when help appeared. At that time there was a fireboat station at the base of Gracie Mansion, the home of New York City's mayor which commands a lovely view of the river, Hell Gate, the run-down Queens factories, and the Lawrence Point power plant. Someone (could it have been the mayor himself?) had seen our plight and dispatched the *James E. Callahan* to come to our aid.

The *James E. Callahan* was an aging but handsome fireboat about one hundred feet long. She glistened (somewhat rustily) in her fire-engine red paint and bristled with polished brass nozzles. Her captain, probably fearing he would ground on the same reef, brought her alongside about fifty yards away from us, and shouted to us through a nonpowered megaphone from his pilot house.

Not to be outdone by the NYFD, New York's Police Department arrived on the scene just about the same time. Two patrol cars bounced into the park on Wards Island, sirens blaring and lights flashing, and a NYPD helicopter zoomed down to hover overhead. Moments later, a police boat arrived also, but it stayed a respectful distance away as if waiting for the Fire Department to flub the job whereupon they could nip in and rescue us

Domino passes under the Triborough Bridge—the Hellgate railroad bridge is in the background—near the spot where *Kittiwake* grounded several years earlier.

Aground Under the Triborough Bridge

from "certain death."

With the sirens ashore and the "whop, whop, whop" of the chopper blades overhead, it was impossible for us to hear the fireboat captain or for him to hear us. As far as we were concerned, we did not want to be rescued. We wanted to be pulled off the reef, and time was critically important. No amount of shooing discouraged the helicopter pilot who, no doubt, took our frantic waving as a sign of further distress. The chopper continued to hover fifty feet overhead.

Despite our inability to hear each other, the *Callahan*'s captain understood what was needed. With his ship stemming the swift current, he ordered a boat lowered. Two firemen, looking ridiculously bulky in large orange life jackets, climbed down into the fifteen-foot red lifeboat. One started the outboard motor and the other took up station in the bow, gripping the gunwhales on either side with white knuckles. A huge manila hawser was passed to them, and they set out to cross the short stretch of turbulent water to pass us the line.

Unfortunately, the firemen failed to grasp the principle of reaching a prescribed destination while crossing a moving body of water. They headed straight for *Kittiwake* but soon fetched up many yards downstream at the end of the hawser, which they had to drop to keep from swamping their lifeboat.

The total scene was beyond belief: the police cars in the park, the helicopter overhead, the river rushing past below, and the fireboat crew game but inept.

While the *Callahan*'s crew overhauled their hawser and their lifeboat motored laboriously upcurrent to her mother ship, the U.S. Coast Guard arrived in the form of a forty-footer that had been dispatched from Governor's Island. It was a good thing they got there when they did, because the police boat's engine chose that moment to stop running. As the current swept the police boat toward Mill Rock (a tiny island in the middle of the river), the

Aground Under the Triborough Bridge

Coast Guard sped to their side, passed them a line, and towed them to safety out of sight up the Harlem River.

Now the *Callahan* was ready for another try. Again the lifeboat struck out across the abyss that separated *Kittiwake* from her would-be rescuers, and again the current swept them downstream before they even got close to us. Helpless observers, the three of us on *Kittiwake* could hardly contain our laughter, the ludicrous nature of the situation overpowering whatever anxiety we may have felt over our predicament.

By this time the helicopter had retired to a safe altitude, but it still kept watch from a distance. The police had turned off their flashing lights and were lounging against the front fenders of their cars taking a smoke break while they watched.

With the lifeboat back alongside, the *Callahan*'s captain held a conference with his crew. We could see gesturing and pointing (in an upcurrent direction). This time they got it right. They headed well upstream of *Kittiwake* and reached us with no difficulty. We were ready. Grasping the hawser we took it aft to the winches, and wrapped a line of our own around it at the bow in lieu of our bow chocks which the line was too large to pass through. We dug *Kittiwake*'s axe out of her emergency gear in case we had to cut the hawser, and at a signal from Barney, the *Callahan* steamed out into the river giving a mighty heave on the hawser. *Kittiwake* turned 180 degrees on her keel, the hawser lifted from the river, droplets of water spun from it as it took the strain, and the massive line parted with a dull thud a few feet in front of *Kittiwake*'s bow. The four-inch diameter hawser was rotten all the way through!

The *James E. Callahan* pulled in the remains of her hawser and retired in disgrace to her pier. Their efforts were appreciated, but their ineptitude and the condition of their gear was appauling. We were thankful we weren't in *real* danger!

Aground Under the Triborough Bridge

The Coast Guard reappeared out of the Harlem River a short time later. They came alongside, asked if we were in any difficulty or if anyone was hurt, and when we assured them we were okay they told us to sit tight. They would be back when the tide came in again.

With that they motored off toward Governors Island. The helicopter whisked away toward Queens, and eventually the patrolmen got bored and moved on. We were alone, except for the thousands of cars passing overhead, in the shadow of the Triborough Bridge.

Later, we learned from a friend that he had heard about us on one of New York's continuous news radio stations. In a "... and this bulletin just handed me ..." statement the announcer told New York that three men were stranded on a yacht sinking in the East River. At that moment we were not sinking, we were doing just the opposite.

Our situation wasn't too bad. Our two worst problems were hunger and the embarrassment of sitting there being gawked at in a city of eight million people. We had not been able to get any sandwiches before leaving Brooklyn, and a thorough search of *Kittiwake*'s lockers failed to turn up a single can of food. Barney and Humphrey had carefully removed every scrap of food before leaving Copenhagen. Barney and I had each smuggled aboard fifty bottles of Tuborg *Grøen*. Humphrey said he had some vintage wine and some caviar aboard, but he was damned if we were going to get into any of that. So we broke into the beer's hiding place and each drank a bottle of very warm Tuborg. It seemed to help.

By now the tide had gone out a lot more, and *Kittiwake* was listing markedly with her port rail awash. The three of us perched on the high side as if sailing to windward in a force-five wind. Except for the slight apprehension about what the high tide would bring we were okay. There was plenty of action to watch including occasional river traffic, multitudes of cars traveling over the

Aground Under the Triborough Bridge

bridge and down the East River Drive, and kids trying to reach us with rocks thrown from the Wards Island shore.

After a while we noticed a small white outboard-powered boat heading our way. As it approached we could see that it was a Coast Guard vessel with two young, uniformed seamen in it. For a long time they motored around us, moving back and forth in the river's current until we waved to them and beckoned them to come alongside. They were reluctant, at first, until we assured them that there was plenty of water for their small boat. When they got closer we asked them what they were doing.

"We've been sent out to keep an eye on you," they said.

"Why don't you tie up and come aboard?" we suggested.

"Well... we don't know if we ought to do that." It was said as if we were mysterious visitors from outer space or were suspected of carrying the plague.

"Look, we argued, all you're doing is wasting gasoline motoring around like that. We're going to be here for hours. You probably don't even have enough gasoline to last. Throw us a line, and tie up."

We finally talked them into it. The two Coast Guardsmen joined us on the rail, and after more persuasion each of them had a beer. They were very young—reservists on weekend patrol they said—and we enjoyed the diversion that their company provided. We spent several hours talking until they got nervous that the forty-footer might return and catch them fraternizing with the enemy. They climbed back into their outboard boat and motored away.

About seven o'clock the forty-footer did come back. They passed us a line (about half the size of the *Callahan*'s hawser and nylon rather than manila) which we passed through the bow chocks and secured to a winch as before. When their first few attempts to pull us off failed, I began to have that sinking feeling that we might be stuck for good, but eventually *Kittiwake* began to grind along the ledge and then she bobbed free.

Aground Under the Triborough Bridge

They came alongside and towed us to quieter water behind Mill Rock while Humphrey gave them the necessary information for their assistance report. Then *Kittiwake*'s engine fired into life, and we were once more on our way, passing through Hell Gate with a favorable current. Humphrey disappeared below.

"To hell with it," he said, clutching his vintage wine and precious caviar when he reappeared in the hatch. "We're going to celebrate."

III

A Cruise Down the Inland Waterway

On one of those particularly harried and frustrating afternoons early one summer, I returned to the office with fifteen phone messages from at least a dozen people I didn't have time to talk with. One of them was from a Mr. Church in somewhere New Hampshire whom I was *sure* I didn't have time to talk with. I didn't know any "Mr. Church" and therefore returning his call could lead to nothing better than an addition to too many activities I was already juggling. Nevertheless, being a "good soul" at heart and because I am by nature curious, I called operator 6 in Watchamacallit, New Hampshire and asked for Mr. Church. Was I glad I did!

As a matter of fact, I didn't know Mr. Church, but I knew his wife; she was Lucia Thwaits, with whom I had learned to sail in the Meteor Class on Manhasset Bay back in the late 1940s. Coincidentally, I had just put the final period on my "Dogwatch" column for *Yacht Racing* in which I recounted some of the good old days in the Meteors (see Chapter XIII), and here was one of my old buddies and sister of one of my sailing instructors on the phone to say "Hi" after more than twenty years.

Lucia and Peter Church lived in a log cabin seventy-eight hundred feet high in the shadow of Pikes Peak near Colorado Springs. They both had been re-bitten by the

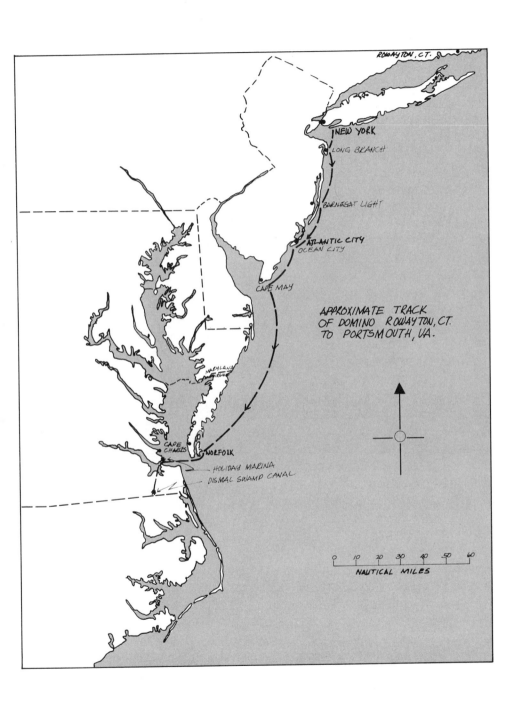

A Cruise Down the Inland Waterway

sailing bug during a winter Caribbean charter, and wanted to buy a cruising boat. Cascade, Colorado and a cruising sailboat are about as unlikely a combination as one can imagine. They planned to take a year's leave of absence from Peter's job starting in June and just go sailing. They had found a boat that they liked and at the insistence of "Ma" Thwaits had gone to great trouble to find their old friend Teddy Jones who "is still fooling around with boats" somewhere in Connecticut—at least he was ten years ago when they last received a Christmas card. Well, anyway, here was Lucia on the phone asking me if I would give them some advice on buying a boat, called *Domino,* which they had found in Essex, Connecticut.

With all the pressing things on my mind I said, "Why not!" and an adventure began.

Domino was purchased in spite of a few deficiencies turned up by John Atkin's thorough survey. We took delivery of her for Lucia and Pete and turned her over to Grove Ely's Boatworks in Rowayton to make her fit for a sea voyage and a year's cruising in the tropics.

It was fun spending someone else's money for a change instead of my own. Before we knew it, *Domino* had stayed most of the summer in Grove's care, but she was in all respects ready for sea.

Being essentially neophytes, the Churches asked my wife Dorcas and me if we'd help them take *Domino* to Fort Lauderdale. The pressing problems of the summer being things of the past we said, again, "Why not!"

The Joneses are not cruising people. Sailboat racing is our thing, and we've found that even when we have tried to go cruising it's been done on a racing schedule leaving us all rather breathless at the end but no less enthusiastic for sailing no matter what its form. The thought of doing the Inland Waterway had long lingered as a project of the future, and it was with great anticipation that we embarked.

Having heard so much about the Waterway—both

The author's shipmates, tired of hearing him belittle their estimates of wave heights, labeled this gale-driven beauty off the entrance to Chesapeake Bay a "Jones two-footer."

good and bad—for many years, I was just a little skeptical about its charms. In fact, I was prepared to be a bit bored by it all. The *Waterway Guide* is pretty glowing about *all* of it. It couldn't be that good, I mused, and put a lot of the glow down to PR. Having raced to Bermuda and from Bermuda to Copenhagen among other like adventures, and having helped deliver Charlie Morgan's twelve-meter *Heritage* (hardly the world's most luxurious cruising yacht) outside all the way from Fort Lauderdale to Connecticut (Chapter I) I can be forgiven, perhaps, for being slightly jaded. I was in for a surprise. The Waterway is everything, as beautiful, as demanding, as relaxing, as varied, as absolutely fabulous as the *Waterway Guide* says it is.

Through no fault of The Boatworks, *Domino* was not quite ready for sea. I knew the wiring was not very good, but since Peter is an engineer and expert electrician I figured I'd leave that department to him to fiddle with during those boring days on the Waterway. Peter took one look and spent the next week rewiring *Domino* while she sat at The Boatworks' dock in Five Mile River. It was okay with me as I still had a week's work to do ashore, but it did take away our contingency time that we'd hoped we could spend with Lucia's parents at Key Biscayne at the end of the trip.

Finally, Peter announced the wiring sufficiently straightened out but by no means to his complete satisfaction. We could depart, which we did at 0842, Wednesday, October 21. It was a cold, clear, beautiful fall day, but windless, which was all to the good as we still had some last-minute but very necessary chores to perform.

We took a final check on the compass by swinging known ranges to and from Green's Ledge light. We picked up two life rafts from our boat *Trilogy* which was on a mooring in Greenwich. We swung Peter's new RDF at Execution Rocks, which had been a landmark for Lucia and me when we were kids; and only when this final chore was performed and we headed for the Throg's Neck

A Cruise Down the Inland Waterway

Bridge (which wasn't there when we were kids) did we all feel that we were officially under way.

At noon we settled down to do some sightseeing down the East River and past the Manhattan skyline; all except Peter, that is, who had found a deck leak and decided that this might be the last opportunity to fix it. I didn't object since the leak was over my bunk. So while the rest of us ogled the incredulous New Yorkers who ogled us, Peter bent to his task of re-bedding the molding between deck and cabin house.

At 1735 we departed Roamer Shoal in Lower Bay and set a compass course for Sandy Hook. Our plan was to make the necessary first outside leg down the New Jersey coast to Cape May and then, weather permitting, make a quick outside hop to Norfolk, thereby saving the one hundred miles and the several days it would take us to go up Delaware Bay and down the Chesapeake. There was still no wind as we passed Sandy Hook at dusk so we continued under power, setting watches for the night at 1900.

Inexplicably, the binnacle light wouldn't go on, so Peter had some more emergency work to do, hooking up a light with a spare dry-cell battery. Later, we discovered that the binnacle and the engine blower were somehow interconnected. With the binnacle on and the blower off, the binnacle would light and the blower would run at low speed. With the blower switched on, the blower ran at full speed and the binnacle light went out! More wiring problems for Peter.

In spite of an early morning fog and no wind, we reached Cape May at 1400 Thursday to take on fuel and check the weather forecast for our proposed outside sail to Norfolk.

After we had taken on fuel a very strong odor of gasoline remained in the cabin, and we delayed our departure until the fumes could be cleared. We had not closed the main hatch (which we should have), and surmised that the strong wind, which had now sprung up from the east, had blown the fumes down the hatch. We were later to discover differently.

The weather forecaster that I reached on the phone at the Norfolk Weather Bureau office was not much help. Unlike most forecasters I have encountered who are helpful and courteous, this one was surly and uncooperative. He read the weather reports to me, but refused to give any opinion of expected weather or any interpretation of the forecast. Nevertheless, what he read encouraged us to try the outside route to Norfolk.

We departed Cape May at 1647, setting sail for the first time. Peter and I went below to get some rest before taking the 1900-to-2300 watch. After about fifteen minutes we both went on deck; the gasoline fumes had reappeared and we're getting rapidly worse. It was apparent to both of us that something was seriously wrong and that we would have to discover the source of the gasoline leak.

The engine and carburetor were completely dry. There was no sign of leakage around any of the tank fittings or seams. The fuel lines and filter were dry as well. The deck plate to the fill pipe was removed and inspected; okay. It had to be the fuel-tank vent which meant everything was coming out of the cockpit seat lockers. Sure enough, a hose clamp had rusted through, allowing the vent hose to work off the tank fitting. Every roll *Domino* took was allowing raw gasoline to drip from the tank into the bilge. Peter got out a spare clamp which I installed with some difficulty through a two-inch by three-inch hole in the bulkhead. We turned on the blower (which ran all night before we were satisfied that the odor had gone) and pumped out the bilge. Lucia and Dorcas went below to fix up a cold supper (no stove fire allowed with all that gasoline in the bilge).

The evening was ideal for sailing. There were no stars (our forecast had said it probably would rain on Saturday), but the wind was blowing steadily from the east and we were glad *Domino* was being propelled under sail in the way that was intended.

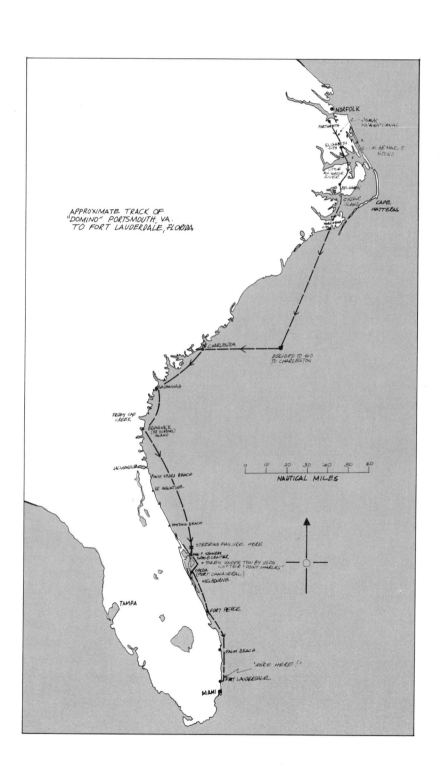

The deck log records that at 0400 it was raining as forecast, our navigation was working out as expected, the fumes were going away, Peter had found a friendly light that we were following on a similar course (it turned out to be the schooner *Agamemnon* making a pilgrimage like ours), and we were, finally, at peace with the world.

The peace didn't last long. Peter and I had a good rest after Dorcas and Lucia relieved us at 0700 Saturday, the twenty-third, but by now the weather began to make unpleasant noises. During the morning the wind had increased and the sea was up. It was still below twenty, as forecast, but it was obviously increasing. Dorcas suggested taking in the mainsail before she and Lucia turned in, which I thought was an excellent suggestion, particularly as it was punctuated by a puff close to thirty knots that combined with a large wave to send *Domino* reeling off course and rounding up into the wind in a near broach. Dorcas and Lucia had handed the mizzen and the number-two genoa earlier, so we wallowed under bare poles while the number-two genoa was reset.

The only thing the log entry notes at 1300 is "WET!!!" The rain was lashing us and stinging like hail as the wind tried to drive it through our oilskins. It was succeeding in mine; the log notation of "WET!!!" is in my handwriting.

Our log entry at 1420 as we cleared the bridge-tunnel at the entrance to Chesapeake Bay is followed by the notation "Busy!*" . . . and at the bottom:

"*Winds up to 50 knots, mizzen down, main down, change #2 genoa to working jib; blew out working jib; change to storm jib—seas building to 3–5 ft. (TAJ) rain very heavy at times. Wet!!"

The reason for the "TAJ" following the wave height is I was accused of underestimating wave heights—they really aren't as high as one thinks they are—and my shipmates all felt that they were anywhere from six to fifteen feet!

It was as exciting an afternoon as I have ever spent.

Peter Church, *Domino*'s owner and captain, guides her through the Dismal Swamp Canal. The trees on each side overhang the banks as if to brush the rigging.

The working jib blew itself to ribbons, as I accidentally jibed while trying to assist Peter in starting the drowned engine while also trying to steer into Norfolk harbor which was virtually invisible in the driving rain. It is more than a slight understatement that we did not like being without sail or power at the entrance to one of the world's busiest harbors in the middle of a gale and, due to an oversight on my part, with no detail harbor chart aboard. This was not exactly the fun or leisurely part of our cruise.

Dorcas and Lucia made the speediest headsail change I have ever seen, getting the remains of the jib down and the storm jib up. At least we could sail if we didn't run into land or a supertanker or a submarine. Peter finally coaxed the engine to life, and we hove into the Holiday Marina in Portsmouth at 1900 shivering with cold and wet, tired and hungry but blessedly happy to be safely tied to the dock.

Our offshore friends aboard *Agamemnon* came in safely a few hours later, but with horror tales of their own. We introduced ourselves, poured life-restoring drinks for all hands, and listened to the gale as it screamed itself to death in *Domino*'s staunch rigging.

Sunday, October 24, was a bright, warm, pleasant day. We took advantage of it to dry out and recover our wits from Saturday's gale. It was anyway too late to depart when we finally struggled out of our bunks and had breakfast. We wanted to take the Dismal Swamp route to Elizabeth City, and there was insufficient time to make the complete forty-mile run before dark. Sunday was spent doing chores—putting the rub-rail on the dinghy, removing the unused winch from the boom that touched the dinghy when the boom was lowered, rewiring the binnacle and blower switches, etc. We also swapped sea-stories with others—some less fortunate than us—about experiences of the day before.

At 0820 Monday, October 25, we left the Holiday Marina and chugged past scores of ships, bridges, and com-

A Cruise Down the Inland Waterway

mercial traffic as we headed for the official beginning of the Inland Waterway. The concentration of heavy industry, shipyards, scrap yards, and railroads is fascinating if not particularly beautiful, and the challenge of threading one's way through tight quarters, under bridges and dodging tugboats is more than enough to keep one's interest.

It is here that you get the first opportunity—a necessity—to use whistle signals. You think twice when the big tug that's coming up from astern at twelve knots gives you two short blasts. You dive for the horn and fumble through the pages of the *Waterway Guide* to make sure you remembered correctly, and belatedly give him two feeble honks in reply. Thereafter, the horn lives on deck and you don't have to refer to the book to refresh your memory. Whistle signals become a matter of routine.

Just before 0930 we went through a final swing bridge and were suddenly in wilderness—well, almost. A sharp right turn after passing under the fixed highway bridge put us into the entrance to the Dismal Swamp Canal. We pulled up at the lock just in time to miss getting in with a group of yachts that were locking up to the canal's higher water level.

The log indicates that we were nearly an hour getting through the lock, but there was so much that was new to all of us about locking that the time did not drag. The whole process was fascinating.

We locked through with six powerboats as very few sailboats take this route due to its controlling depth of only six feet. We enjoyed watching the last boat in, a thirty-four-foot houseboat which was captained by a large grandmotherly type. She handled the controls expertly and gave precise commands to a less large grandfatherly type who handled lines aft. We were later to learn that these pleasant people were the Harrisons. Mr. Harrison called across the lock to tell us to be sure to ask the lockmaster at the end of the canal for some honey which he usually sold and which was very good. The Harrisons had obviously been this way before.

A Cruise Down the Inland Waterway

The *Waterway Guide* says that George Washington surveyed the Dismal Swamp Canal and that it is the oldest canal in the U.S. It is very narrow—seeming hardly wide enough for two boats to pass—and runs dead straight for twenty miles where it jogs left and runs dead straight for another twenty miles to the south lock.

Rather than being a bore as one would think, this straight line running seemingly in the middle of nowhere —unfathomable leagues from the sea where *Domino* belonged—was breathtakingly beautiful. Even the light rain didn't dampen our spirits; and when we met the Pierces, who have made the Dismal Swamp Canal their only route in six years of cruising south in their Newporter ketch, they confirmed that they never tired of this part of the trip.

The North Carolina woods grow right to the edge of the canal. The trees seem to brush the spars. Here and there one can see parts of the original wood bulkheads built in George Washington's time. Lake Drummond's side canal beckons for exploration—although we didn't have the time to stop.

Dorcas's words in the log summed it up for all of us: "Dismal Swamp Canal is a really groovy ditch!!!"

After leaving the straight canal, the Pasquotank River widens and winds its way to Elizabeth City where we tied up at Maritime Services Texaco Marina. Here again we saw the Pierces who lived aboard their forty-foot Newporter the year around, taking her South in the fall and North in the spring. Our formal introduction was the next morning when Mr. Pierce came padding down the dock in his bare feet clutching a bundle of aluminum foil.

"Still hot," he said, holding it aloft. I must have looked puzzled. "My wife just baked some bread and it's still hot. Thought you might like some for breakfast."

Imagine baking bread on a forty-foot sailboat! But Mrs. Pierce does it every other day, and the excess goes to the marina operators and whomever happens to be lucky

Domino's crew did not let a light drizzle dampen their enthusiasm for the Dismal Swamp Canal as they waited to be locked through to the Pasquotank River.

A Cruise Down the Inland Waterway

enough to be tied up nearby. We were to soon learn that such uncommon folk as the Pierces and the Harrisons are more common on the Waterway than elsewhere. Their presence makes the trip just that much more enjoyable.

Domino spent two days in Elizabeth City while I flew home to some brief business, and then we were off once more.

We set sail for the first time since the gale, catching and passing the Pierces to get even for their passing us in the canal. The Pasquotank widens as it nears Albermarle Sound which we had to cross to reach the Alligator River where the main channel of the Waterway rejoins our Dismal Swamp route.

We anchored in six feet of water in a sheltered cove of the Little Alligator River. The Pierces came in also but couldn't enter as far as we because of their deeper draft.

Saturday, October 30, we again got an early start in the fog. Our course took us into Pamlico Sound closer to the coast and then into the Neuse River where we set *Domino*'s spinnaker and ran under sunshine, both seen for the first time, to the inlet that would lead us to Morehead City and the sea.

We anchored that night in Cedar Creek, a small cove off the main Waterway channel, which has to be one of the most beautiful anchorages I have ever visited. We launched the dinghy and took turns sailing into the Creek until we were treated to a spectacular sunset which was, in turn, followed by a silent, enchanting evening.

An equally spectacular sunrise had us up and moving at 0735 Sunday morning, and we pulled into Morehead City for supplies at 1000.

It was necessary to go outside from here in order to make up some time.

The wind was again from the east at fifteen knots and we had good, but lumpy, going. This was theoretically ideal as it would speed us on our way to Florida, but it was rough and uncomfortable for our smooth-water-accus-

Domino riding placidly at anchor in Cedar Creek, just above Moorehead City, the night before venturing forth into the ocean on her outside passage to Charleston.

tomed stomachs. A dinner went over the side (I'll never tell whose), but we pressed on, passing Frying Pan Shoal light at 0124 Monday morning, November first—the day we were supposed to be in Florida.

The wind went southeast and lightened at dawn, and before long it was down to five knots and southwest—on the nose. Conditions did not look favorable. We hadn't been able to stock our larder in Moorehead City as thoroughly as we had wished, so we gave up on Key Biscayne and headed inshore for Charleston.

From Charleston, we went into the Waterway again and found that it is quite different in this area from North Carolina. Whereas in North Carolina the water is mostly fresh with no tides or currents, below Charleston it is formed through saltwater inlets where the tide range is high and the current swift.

Our friendly weatherman promised a cold frontal passage in a day or so with little promise of wind until it passed. We took advantage of the lull to run day and night —setting watches as we would at sea. We found several lights extinguished and managed to hit bottom when we cut a channel marker too close.

"But we can't be aground, we're in the middle of a city," mumbled an incredulous Peter as he stumbled out of his bunk, awakened from a sound sleep at 0100. But we most certainly were! We launched the dinghy into the swift current (falling tide, too), and Dorcas rowed our anchor out into deep water. We blew the circuit breaker from overloading the electric windlass, but after a bit of manual cranking on the Barient #30 and grinding full speed on the engine, *Domino* slid into deep water, thereby avoiding the embarrassment of treating the residents of Beaufort, S.C., to the spectacle of a stranded sailboat as they went off to work in the morning.

Dawn brought us a sunny day and we motored through Savannah, Georgia, unconcerned and taking in the many and interesting sights. It wasn't until we were

A Cruise Down the Inland Waterway

well past Savannah that we began to think of a fuel stop; but when I consulted the *Waterway Guide* I found to my dismay that there weren't any!

A quick measure of the fuel supply led me to the conclusion that we might make it to Saint Simon's Island, Georgia, and then again we might not. The only possible alternative was a little town named Valona which the *Waterway Guide* listed as a possible source of mechanical help in an emergency. We discovered that Valona was a shrimp town. We went up the creek to the village at sunset as the shrimpers were coming in. There was no marked channel, but we figured where they could go we could go also. We tried to remember which side to favor in which bends so we could get out again. Such a town must have a gas station, we reasoned, and we could ferry our jerry cans out in the dinghy if all else failed.

We tied up to a shrimper and got the once-over as if we were travelers from outer space. They were helpful and friendly, however; but the sad news was that the nearest gasoline station was seventeen miles up the road and that at the moment everyone was unloading, culling, and packing the day's catch of shrimp. We would get no help here!

Out into the night again with the engine throttled down for our best guess at maximum cruise. The night was pitch black, the channel was narrow and winding, several more lights were extinguished, and we became more and more apprehensive. Setting watches was out of the question as it took all of us to con the ship. One was continually navigating—setting compass courses between each mark, interpreting channels and ranges, and making time/distance calculations; one of us was steering with one eye glued to the compass and the other glued to range lights (try this sometime when running a stern range); the other two were searching in the gloom for unlighted channel markers.

We couldn't keep this pace up for long. Nor had we

A Cruise Down the Inland Waterway

forgotten about our dwindling gasoline supply. A glance at the chart at about 2130 showed a very difficult passage ahead. I could see no way we could navigate it in the dark without a generous supply of luck. Added to all the other problems, the current was running fast and unpredictably, threatening to take us off course and into shallow water. Only the ranges had kept us from running aground up to now.

The chart also showed a cove off the channel just before we reached the difficult stretch. It would not be easy to get in; but, once in, there would be plenty of water and room to swing at anchor. Also, we would be out of the channel completely, thereby avoiding the possibility of being run down by someone else running at night. Unlikely, but an unpleasant possibility.

We pulled into Fridaycap Creek at 2215. Wouldn't you know that the range that marked our turning point was out, not only making our entrance difficult, but also making the narrow passage down the channel impossible to negotiate should we have tried to do so.

Our relief to be safely anchored was increased by the arrival of the northwest wind which we knew would follow the frontal squall line that had passed through the previous afternoon. It meant that we could once again sail offshore—making better time—but, more important, we could sail to Saint Simon's Island (albeit with difficulty) if our gasoline ran out.

At 0700 Thursday, November 4, we bade a grateful farewell to Fridaycap Creek (suddenly one of our all-time favorite anchorages) and headed downwind and downcurrent to Olsen's Marina on Lanier Island (across the bridge from Saint Simon's Island) where we filled up with thirty-eight gallons in a forty-gallon tank.

By 1100 we were on our way again, leaving all the powerboats tied up at Olsen's as it was too windy for them to venture out. The wind was from the north at twenty knots.

Once outside, we set the number-one and number-

A Cruise Down the Inland Waterway

two genoas with the number one set on the spinnaker pole to windward. It was an effective twin headsail arrangement and *Domino* reeled off the knots.

By 2200 we were abeam of Saint Augustine—Florida at last! By 0500 the next morning we were abeam of Ponce de Leon Light.

It was Peter's and my turn to have the long night with the two four-hour watches. When Lucia and Dorcas came on deck at 0700 I was so exhausted I didn't even wait to eat breakfast, but went straight to my bunk.

I was nearly asleep when I heard Dorcas call down that there was something funny about the steering. "Just steer the boat and let me get some sleep," I shouted. When she was quite insistent on her second call, I stumbled on deck and discovered that we had, indeed, lost all control of the rudder. It was no longer connected to the wheel. Damn! What next?

We were in no immediate danger. Our course was still directly downwind, and although there were hazardous shoals extending out from Cape Canaveral just ahead, we could easily keep outside of them.

While Dorcas and Lucia took in the mainsail, Peter and I inspected the steering situation to see if we could make emergency repairs. I had noted before we left that some previous owner had removed *Domino*'s emergency steering rig as it interfered with where the helmsman sat. There was nothing to do about it, however, particularly now.

The steering quadrant which attached the cables to the rudder was broken off. No possibility of repair at sea!

I was not concerned with our immediate safety, but Peter and Lucia wore long faces. We were in no danger as yet, but I thought it a good idea to notify the Coast Guard that we were out there and that we would perhaps require assistance. We raised Ponce de Leon Coast Guard with some difficulty—Peter discovered some loose connections in the newly installed antenna and had to correct the problem first.

Ponce de Leon Coast Guard informed us that they had an eighty-two-foot cutter in Port Canaveral if we needed it. A few quick calculations indicated that at our present rate of four knots we would not arrive at Fort Pierce until early the next morning. We could get into a lot of trouble in the meantime; and, once there, it would still be difficult if not impossible to maneuver in the inlet. We accepted the Coast Guard's implied offer of assistance, and in no time we were tied up at their dock in Port Canaveral, tired but safe.

I cannot say enough for the skipper and crew of the *Point Charles* who came out to tow us in. They handled their boat and ours in a highly professional manner. It is very comforting to know they are there when you need them.

A friendly machine shop brazed our quadrant together, and we were on our way in the morning. We returned to the inside route so as not to strain our questionable steering gear, and by so doing we discovered one of the most delightful stretches of the Waterway, the Alligator River.

The rest of the trip to Fort Lauderdale was an anticlimax. With renewed confidence in our ability to steer, we went outside again at Fort Pierce Inlet and arrived at Pier 66, Fort Lauderdale, at 0045 Monday morning, November 8. The log reports, "What a nifty sail to end the voyage."

"We're here!!!"

One trip on the Inland Waterway deserves another. It is impossible to appreciate everything that is to be seen and it is impossible to see it all.

We learned many things, not the least of which was that cruising isn't necessarily any duller than racing. This, the companionship of good friends, the opportunity to meet new ones, and the satisfaction of getting *Domino* safely south, made the trip a highlight of a lifetime afloat.

IV

Record Passage

THE 1971 MIAMI TO MONTEGO Bay race is relatively easy for me to recall. I did it aboard Mark Johnson's *Windward Passage*—already a legend at that time, and we were to add yet another classic victory to her impressive accomplishments. I was aboard not as a regular crew member, but as a photographer—to do a documentary film—so I have an hour-long record of the race which I have reviewed probably a hundred times, showing the film to various sailing audiences.

Windward Passage was designed by Alan P. Gurney for Robert W. Johnson. Gurney's *Guinevere* had won the 1967 Southern Ocean Racing Conference under her owner, the late George M. Moffett, Jr., and Johnson was impressed—not only by *Guinevere*'s win but also by the attitude of her young English designer. In contrast to some of the more established design offices of that time, Gurney was receptive to some of Johnson's revolutionary ideas, willing—even anxious—to try them out.

Johnson owned the L. Francis Herreshoff-designed *Ticonderoga* at the time he approached Gurney for a new design. *Ticonderoga* was herself a legendary yacht even before Johnson bought her, and under the Oregon lumber tycoon she continued her winning ways and set course records all over the world. "Big Ti" is a large yacht, one of the "maxis," so-called because they are at the top of the

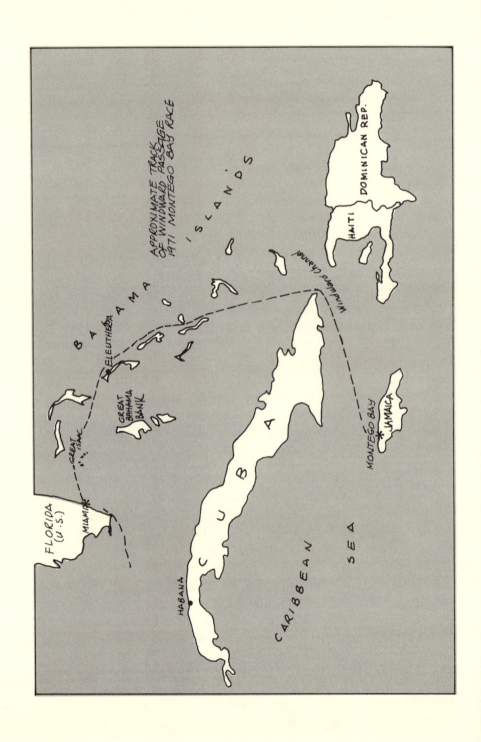

Record Passage

seventy-three-foot size limit in force for most ocean races. With her, Johnson learned the joys of finishing first and setting course records, but *Ti* was an old yacht and had her limitations.

In her replacement, Johnson wanted an even faster yacht, still within the size limit imposed by the measurement rule, with which he could continue finishing first and breaking course records. He wasn't concerned with the handicap rating, he wanted to be first in. If a smaller boat won on corrected time, that would be okay. Gurney was to design the fastest possible yacht that could be built within seventy-three-foot perpendiculars.

Since Johnson was in the lumber business, it was natural for him to want his new yacht to be built of wood. The first thought was a multi-chine, plywood planked hull, and, in fact, a full set of lines were developed for this hull. The final design was, however, a more conventional round bilge hull built of three diagonal layers of cedar over a framework of bulkheads and stringers. A resident and citizen of the Bahamas, Johnson set up his own boatyard in Freeport, Grand Bahama, to build the boat.

The new yacht's hull shape was very much like a dinghy. We had a good laugh when Alan Gurney met Bruce Kirby, editor of *One-Design & Offshore Yachtsman* magazine and designer of several highly successful International-14 dinghies. Alan and Bruce spread out their plans in the back of the magazine's booth at the New York Boat Show, and the sections of the two designs were almost identical—except that one was fourteen-feet long and the other almost seventy-three! The Gurney design was indeed radical for her time, being extremely beamy (nineteen feet) and having a very low displacement (eighty thousand pounds) for her waterline length (sixty-five feet).

Alan told me two amusing stories about the building of Johnson's yacht. The keel, which is lead and designed to weigh 33,800 pounds, was made by fabricating a wooden pattern which was placed in a box and surrounded by sand. The pattern, box, and sand were then buried in the ground, and when the pattern was removed, the molten lead was poured into the sand cavity to assume the shape of the keel when the lead cooled.

This is a mammoth undertaking—melting and pouring thirty-four thousand pounds of lead—and when over thirty-six thousand pounds had been poured without filling the mold, Johnson called Gurney at his New York office.

"We've poured over thirty-six thousand pounds," Johnson told Gurney. "You'd better re-check your figures and tell us how much lead is supposed to go into that hole."

Gurney, always a meticulous designer, didn't doubt his figures, but acknowledged that a mistake was possible. He double-checked the volume of the keel design, and it came out as before—33,800 pounds. Gurney called Johnson back and after much persuasive argument convinced Johnson that something had gone wrong with their pouring operation and to suspend it. Sure enough, when the lead had cooled and the mold was dug out of the ground, it was found that the massive weight of the molten lead had split the bottom of the box, and approximately 5,000 pounds of lead had seeped into the ground surrounding the mold. The whole process had to be started over—36,000 pounds of solid lead had to be cut into small pieces and then melted down again. The second keel-pouring was successful, and the finished casting weighed almost exactly 33,800 pounds.

When the new yacht was launched, she was christened *Windward Passage,* a rather strange-sounding name then (although we have become used to it now), for the notoriously turbulent stretch of water between Cuba and Haiti known as the Windward Passage. Johnson could not completely fit *Passage* in the Bahamas, and she was to sail to Spencer's yard in West Palm Beach for the

Mark Johnson's 73-foot "maxi" *Windward Passage* close-hauled at 10-plus knots shortly after the start of the Miami-Montego Bay, Jamaica Race.

Record Passage

final finishing touches. Bob Johnson invited the designer to come down for the eighty-mile trip from Grand Bahama Island across the Gulf Stream to Florida.

I happened to have lunch with Gurney the day before he was to make the trip. Alan is usually a laconic person —given to few words none of which do much to reveal any deep inner conflicts, doubts, or emotions if, in fact, any exist. He is a very experienced ocean racer, by that time having sailed two transatlantic races as well as several Fastnet, Bermuda, SORC, and numerous lesser races, and he had designed many ocean-racing yachts including one of the largest, most daring "maxi" racers ever attempted. When we returned from lunch and were looking at the plans of *Windward Passage* spread out on his drafting table, Alan said with a revealing introspection: "You know, Ted, I'm really looking forward to this trip." And he added, chuckling as he said the words, "I've never sailed on a seventy-three-footer."

As is now well documented, *Windward Passage* quickly established herself as an outstanding boat. They had some bad moments during her first Saint Petersburg to Fort Lauderdale race when *Passage*'s flat, dinghylike hull pounded badly in the heavy seas of the Gulf Stream off Florida's Key West. She shook so badly that her designer was beginning to doubt that he'd made her strong enough—surely she would shake herself to pieces, Alan thought. Then he suggested to Johnson that they add sail to make her heel and sail more on her lines. That did it. She not only went faster, but the pounding stopped. She was beaten in that race by Ted Turner's converted 12-Meter *American Eagle,* but *Passage* went on, in her first few months, to break the Miami-Nassau and Miami-Montego Bay race records. From Jamaica she sailed west and broke the course record in the Honolulu race which Johnson had set with *Ticonderoga,* but the record was

Record Passage

taken away due to a protest of a minor foul at the starting line. Many wondered how an actual elapsed time record could be stricken by a right-of-way protest, but it was. And then, suddenly, Bob Johnson was dead, the victim of a heart attack.

Windward Passage did not die with Johnson. He had set up a fund to support her campaigns after his death. *Passage* was documented as a U.S. flag vessel but she could not be registered in his name because as a Bahamian citizen he was, technically, an alien and could not own a vessel registered in the U.S. *Windward Passage* had always been registered in the name of Bob's oldest son Mark, who assumed her command.

Because of my close friendship with Alan Gurney, because I had watched *Passage* come to life on his drawing board, and because it would be a unique experience to sail aboard such an unusual sailboat, I wanted to race with Mark to Bermuda in 1970—not just to be a part of the crew, but to record the event on film. I had only met Bob Johnson once, and I had never met Mark, but at Alan's suggestion I wrote to Chip Cleary, who was *Passage*'s "executive officer" and asked if I could go along to do the film. Chip wrote back; no. Crestfallen, I reported my rejection to Alan, who suggested I phone Chip. But Chip was firm. He didn't have any room on the Bermuda Race, even for a noncombatant photographer, but he would be glad to have me aboard for one of the Circuit races (Southern Ocean Racing Conference) or the Jamaica Race the next winter. "Put me down for the Jamaica Race," I told Chip, and that's how I came to be in Miami in March 1971, standing on the dock alongside *Windward Passage* with a duffel bag and fifty pounds of cameras and recording equipment.

Windward Passage's 1969 record in the Miami to Montego Bay race was four days, eleven hours, and fifty-six seconds. The race distance is nominally eight hundred eleven miles which meant that *Passage* had ave-

Record Passage

raged a little better than 7.5 knots. This is excellent speed, but we were, of course, anxious to set a new record if we could. We had a few problems to overcome, not the least of which was a splice in the mainmast where it had been broken in the Lucaya Race a month earlier. A new mast was waiting in California—for the Transpac—and aside from the fact that we couldn't set a course record if the mast broke again, *Passage* needed this mast to get her to the West Coast after sailing to Jamaica.

As race day dawned, another obstacle to a record passage appeared. The wind had been from the east for several days, and it continued from that direction. Not only that, it was forecast to go southerly over the next few days —meaning that we would have to beat all the way to Eleuthera and then very likely beat all the way south to the Windward Passage before being able to ease sheets for Jamaica. It would mean a total of perhaps five hundred miles on the wind, almost impossible to make good better than 7.5 knots sailing to windward over that distance.

When the race started, the wind was fresh from slightly south of east. This was better than due east, but it was a bad sign for breaking the record. Our navigator was Peter Bowker, who had been navigator aboard *Escapade* when the first Jamaica Race record was set—*Ticonderoga* when she broke *Escapade*'s record—and *Windward Passage* when she broke *Ticonderoga*'s record. We had the boat and the navigator and the crew (most of whom had sailed with Bob Johnson) who could do it. All we needed was some cooperation from the weather. Peter was so pessimistic, though, that we all but forgot about a record even when the first course took us to Great Isaac Light on a close fetch.

Mark Johnson had only been skippering *Windward Passage* for a short time, but he made a perfect start. In spite of *Passage*'s dinghy heritage, she cannot be started like a dinghy. She needs a lot of room and time to tack.

With a perfect start near the windward end of the starting line, *Windward Passage* moves out on the fleet as the Miami skyline recedes on the horizon.

Record Passage

You don't whip a seventy-three-footer into a hole in the fleet thirty seconds before the gun—you sail way out from the pack, tack or jibe with two minutes or more to go, and head for the line hoping there will be room when you get there. For these reasons, big boats rarely hit the line with the gun, but this time we did. In a matter of seconds after the start we were in the lead at the favored end of the line speeding away from the fleet. Our only serious rivals for first to finish honors—Huey Long's *Ondine* and Ted Turner's *American Eagle*—were far astern struggling to get through the pack. *Windward Passage* stepped out under number-two jib top, staysail, and full mainsail in a twenty-knot wind making ten knots. In a very few hours only *Ondine* could be seen astern. The rest of the fleet was hull down behind us.

As we entered the north-flowing Gulf Stream, the wind seemed to diminish slightly; and we reset the mizzen (which had been taken down to ease the helm) and replaced the number-two jib top with the number one. As we got more into the Stream, the wind also seemed to let us up slightly—allowing us to ease sheets and increase our speed to eleven knots.

As the sun was setting over our shoulders, Great Isaac Light appeared, and in no time we were whizzing past this lonely looking outpost on a coral rock perched in the middle of the ocean. While I had passed Isaac many times in races from Miami, this was the first time I had seen it in daylight. *Passage* had made the sixty-mile crossing in just six hours to confirm our ten-knot-plus indicated speed.

Peter Bowker had pointed out that this would be a crucial point in the race. After passing Isaac, he plotted a course directly to Great Stirrup Cay (unlike the Miami-Nassau race, there is no requirement to stay north of the reefs between Isaac and Stirrup) which would take us about twenty degrees closer to the wind. Almost as we altered course, the wind came around obligingly, and we

Record Passage

settled down to a night of brisk close, reaching past Great Stirrup Cay and on to Eleuthera.

Dawn revealed *Ondine* hanging doggedly in our wake, but she was nearly hull down—only occasionally showing a burst of bright blue from her topsides. As noon approached, the wind kept veering into the south and then west of south, and the more we were able to ease sheets the more *Ondine* dropped astern. By noon we had a mizzen staysail set, and the speedometer was showing occasional bursts of fourteen knots with sustained speeds over twelve.

Shortly after the change of the watch, Bowker came on deck from the navigator's station and spoke quietly to Mark. "I've just compared our noon position with the Old Man's log, and we're four hours ahead of the (1969) record." Suddenly, with cautious optimism, we had thoughts of breaking the old record, but with almost six hundred miles still to go, it was too early for a celebration.

As we approached Cat Island—almost directly in our path—we elected to pass to its eastward side which Peter calculated would be both shorter and faster. Perhaps sensing that his only chance to catch us was to try for a different slant of wind or current, Huey Long took *Ondine* west of Cat Island. Already just a white speck far astern, she rapidly disappeared from view—the last we were to see of her until after we had reached Jamaica.

The crew of *Windward Passage* had a great respect for the late skipper. He was very much a father figure to many more of them than his own two sons, Mark and Fritz, and the crew often spoke of him as if his ghost were riding with us. If we did something especially well or reached a crucial point—as when *Ondine* disappeared astern—someone would look aloft as if Bob Johnson were perched on the masthead, throw a casual salute and quietly say, "Thanks, Bob." I think some of them really believed that he was smiling down on us from heaven, influencing the gods if he could and cheering us on when we were doing well. When they learned that we were ahead of *Passage*'s old record, one of them shook his fist at the sky and exclaimed, "How do you like that, Bob? We're gonna do it!" And several others took up the cry. It was, in reality, Bob Johnson's spirit that was pushing *Passage* forward. She was, after all, fulfilling the purpose he had envisioned. She was continuing to do what he had created her to do, even after his death. *Windward Passage,* her crew, this race, and the film rolling in my camera were a living tribute to a quiet man who had reveled in fast sailing on the ocean and who had had the guts to go after it all out.

It is easy for an outsider to say, what the hell; he had the money and the time . . . anybody with that much money can do whatever he wants. But while I had never sailed with Bob Johnson and knew him only by reputation, sailing with this crew who knew and loved him I could tell that this had been a special man. We were racing as much for the spirit of Bob Johnson as for ourselves, and somehow I could feel that we would break this record and that *Passage* would go on to the Pacific later that summer and avenge her loss of the Transpac record—which she subsequently did.

We passed Cat Island quickly and boiled along through the southern Bahama Islands with the wind continuing to come aft. By early afternoon we had the mizzen staysail set and by sunset the spinnaker was set and drawing. During the night the wind came around completely, necessitating a jibe to port tack. Toward morning the wind began to lighten, and *Passage*'s speed dropped down to eight or nine knots—the slowest of the trip so far.

At dawn the wind was picking up again, and we changed from the light spinnaker to one of medium cloth weight. Soon we were flying along under spinnaker, full mainsail, and mizzen spinnaker, and once again the speedometer crept past twelve to fourteen, fifteen, then to sixteen, and occasionally seventeen knots. *Windward*

Record Passage

Passage was flying toward her namesake.

As *Passage* exceeds fifteen knots, she starts to rise a "rooster tail" astern in similar fashion to a planing speedboat. Looking over the transom the water swoshes out from under the hull, breaking cleanly without falling back on the transom. As the streams of water from either side of the rudder converge behind the stern, their collision sends a churning froth of white water straight up, obliterating the waves curving aft of the boat. The faster *Passage* sails, above fifteen knots, the further aft the streams of water converge and the higher the rooster tail ... and the noise is considerable. Early that afternoon, we were sending up rooster tails with some regularity.

When Peter Bowker had worked out our noon position, he announced to the crew that we were now twelve hours ahead of the old record. In the first two days we had sailed over 500 miles, making 262 miles the first day and 250 the second. The closer *Windward Passage* got to the Windward Passage, the faster she went, and as we picked up the eastern tip of Cuba in the late afternoon, our speed was almost never below fifteen knots and more often hovering at seventeen.

A large squall threatened just as we were waiting for the word from Peter that it was time to jibe and head for Jamaica. The sky to the east took on a menacing deep purple hue, but it never reached us. However, the wind increased in strength at this time—blowing now perhaps thirty knots true, and when we had completed the jibe *Passage* flew even faster. Although the off-watch had been excused to go below for supper, no one left the deck —it was just too exciting surfing down the waves with the bow wave lifting high on either side and the rooster tail curling away behind us. Shortly after dark we had two surges of speed which put the speedometer needle off the dial. The top speed on the dial is twenty knots.

Earlier, as we approached Point Maisi, Peter took us to within about two miles of the shore line—every mile

Record Passage

east of the point was a mile further to sail to Montego Bay. At that time, relations with Cuba were rather tense, and one of the crew asked the navigator what would happen if a Cuban gunboat came out to see why we were so close to shore. "Don't worry about gunboats," said Peter. "We'll outrun 'em."

At Point Maisi *Windward Passage* was one full day ahead of her time at that position in the race two years previously. We were now twenty-four hours ahead of the record!

We were in the trade winds now with a steady wind from the east-northeast, but the wind lightened slightly during the night until *Passage* was down to an almost sedate ten or eleven knots. In a memo to the crew following the race, Chip Cleary pointed out that this last morning of sailing seemed slow indeed after the exhilarating ride of the night before. Imagine, ten knots in a sailboat seemed *slow.*

Now there was little doubt about breaking the record as long as the mast didn't collapse or some similar disaster didn't overtake us. Spirits were high. We joked with Sandy MacKenzie, the cook, who had put out his galley fire and finally appeared on deck. We kidded Peter Bowker about missing the island, but by late morning the mountains of Jamaica appeared out of the mist, and in the early afternoon we swept across the finish line and into Montego Bay.

Windward Passage broke the old record by thirty-one hours finishing with an elapsed time of three days, three hours, and forty minutes. The average speed for the 811 miles was 10.8 knots which is a higher sustained speed than that achieved by the schooner *Atlantic* when she set the transatlantic record averaging 10.7 knots for twelve days—the highest average speed ever recorded in any of the Atlantic Coast ocean races before *Windward Passage* made her dash for Jamaica.

—And the record still stands!

V

Record Passage In Reverse

I HAD NEVER SAILED WITH Norm Raben. I had sailed with his son, Bruce, when he was a runny-nosed teenager, and we had not gotten along particularly well. I thought he acted rather spoiled; he no doubt missed not having the priviledged status as the owner's kid. He moved around Humphrey Simson's *Kittiwake* (a new Alan Gurney design, replacing the one I had grounded in the East River) with a rather sullen attitude advertising the fact that if he were aboard his father's boat he wouldn't have to do all the lackey work. For his part, he must have looked upon me as the old fart with the overblown reputation who would hog the wheel from those who could steer better, who was too old and feeble to go forward of the mast, and who would disappear as soon as the race was over and the real work began. I suppose there was some justification for both views.

One spring day a couple of years later, Norm called and said that it was time I stopped being a candy ass and got out sailing. He needed crew to race his Gary Mull-designed "flyer," *La Forza del Destino,* to Halifax, Nova Scotia, and I was to come. It wasn't a long race, he would have me back in the office by Monday morning—Tuesday at the latest—so I couldn't use work as an excuse. With that sort of logic and good-natured insult, how could I refuse?

I looked forward to sailing on *La Forza* with mixed

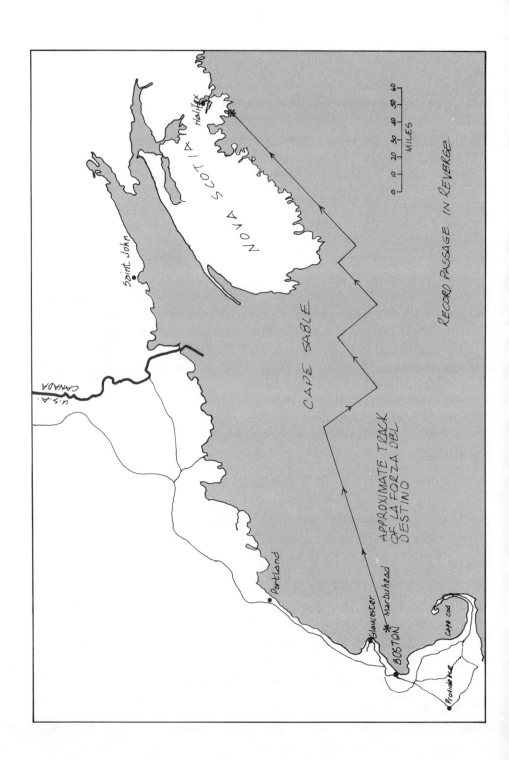

Record Passage In Reverse

emotions. She and her skipper were already legends. They shared the reputation of being flat-out, no-compromise competitors—the boat being created in the man's image. On the one hand, I was anxious to see what made both tick, and to discover how much of the legends were true. On the other hand, I wasn't sure I was up for several days of bashing around the ocean aboard a stripped-out sixty-footer, living in foul-weather gear and eating cold beans. This was to be done with a group of people I didn't know except for the owner and his son, and Bruce and I would have to make some sort of adjustment if the whole thing was to work at all. I wasn't really concerned on the latter score. Bruce was no longer a teenager and had had time to mellow. He had gained a lot of experience since I last sailed with him and had done some impressive things on boats other than *La Forza.* Still, all the unknowns of the situation made me look forward to the end of the race more than to the beginning.

Norm was still short of crew as race-time approached, so I recruited my son Bill (sixteen) who was delighted with the opportunity to make his first real offshore race. But both of us were a bit uneasy as we drove to Marblehead.

Nor was our uneasiness lessened with our arrival. Norm said he would be at a party ashore. We were to take a launch out to *La Forza,* find ourselves bunks, and be ready to get going early the next morning. It was already late when we arrived, so Bill and I went straight out to *La Forza,* not wishing to get involved with the scene at the bar ("Hi, who you sailing with?" *"La Forza."* "Oh, how *is* Raben to sail with?" "Dunno, never sailed with him before." "Aha, are *you* in for a treat!"—the speaker who a minute before knew nothing would be an instant expert as soon as he found out you knew nothing.). Anyway, what do you do with two duffel bags, two pairs of boots, and two sets of foul-weather gear while you socialize? We would at least go out to the boat and get rid of our gear—

Record Passage In Reverse

then think about being social.

La Forza was deserted when we got on board. She was also locked up, which didn't do anything for our enthusiasm quotient. However, we soon found the key in one of the places owners usually hide keys and went below. Fumbling around for the battery switch in the dark, looking around for bunks and lockers that looked available, we soon made ourselves reasonably at home.

I asked Bill if he wanted to go ashore and have a beer or something (he was under age, but we probably could have faked it). "Not really", was his unenthusiastic reply. So we appropriated a couple of bunks and turned in to await whatever adventure, and strange manner of beings, overtook us.

I was awakened by the sound of the radio. My watch read seven o'clock, and I gradually stirred myself into wakefulness. Bill was asleep in his bunk, and there were a couple of other bodies in other bunks snoring contentedly. At the navigator's table was a strange-looking fellow with black hair, an imposing black mustache, and large spectacles. I introduced myself. "Uh, hi" said the mustache and went back to his charts and his radio. I had hoped to get a name, at least, out of the exchange, but he was obviously into something other than conversing with somebody named Jones. Digging around in the galley produced something suitable for breakfast, and so the day had begun.

In due course the sleeping bodies awoke and introduced themselves. I found out that the navigator's name was Jack Harvey. Norm, Bruce, and the balance of the crew arrived, and we set about getting organized for the race, which was to start later in the morning outside the harbor.

It was a lovely, sunny, July day in Marblehead harbor as we went about making *La Forza* ready for sea. However, as often happens in this area at this time of year, outside it was quite foggy. Once under way, the effect of the fog, with the racers and spectators milling close to the race committee boats, was extremely disorienting. Only the wind, the trim of the sails, and the compass—if you were in a place where you could see it—gave a hint of direction. It was as if we were inside an outsized, frosted brandy snifter. We could have been offshore a mile or a hundred. We could have been off Massachusetts or Bora Bora, except that I suppose there is never any fog around Bora Bora.

The wind was light, about eight knots, from the northeast, and Jack told us that we would not quite be able to lay the rhumb line. Our strategy would be to hold toward Nova Scotia on the starboard tack, which was favored, and see what developed. The long-range forecast was not promising; there was a large area of relatively stable weather which wasn't expected to change appreciably over the next few days.

Norm took the wheel for the start and asked me to stand by with him to advise on tactics. He especially wanted me to keep an eye on our chief rivals, Paul Adams' *Safari* and Dave Steere's *Yankee Girl,* both of which were near our size—among the largest and fastest yachts in the fleet.

This was a special race for *La Forza.* She had twice before won it, and Norm was hopeful of getting the "hat trick" with a third win. Also, it was well known that Norm's real estate business was suffering the fate of many similar developments in the economic crunch of the early 70s, and while there was no discussion of the subject, it was believed that this might well be Norm's last race with *La Forza.* In fact, it was.

We agreed that the only place to start was at the windward (east) end of the line, as that seemed to be heavily favored. Naturally, the other boats in our class wanted to start there also, so the trick was to tread the fine line between barging and being too far down the line, between being early and taking many hours of backwind.

Record Passage In Reverse

I was not aware of a slight current setting us toward the line until it was too late. I had urged Norm to tack in front of *Safari* thinking that we would hit the line with the gun, but it was soon obvious that we would be early. It was obvious to *Safari*'s crew as well, and they successfully blocked our efforts to bear off to kill speed. If we headed up they would be able to squeeze us out at the line. We were boxed! With no place else to go, we crossed the line with a full rap about a boatlength before the gun and had to return.

The spectator fleet had crowded in toward the mark boat to get a better view in the fog, and we caught them completely by surprise as Norm spun *La Forza*'s wheel to tack around and start again. With much shouting, horn honking, and engine revving, the spectator craft scattered before us like chickens fleeing the fox. How we managed to miss any is a minor miracle, and I wouldn't have been surprised if several of the spectator boats had collided in their frantic efforts to get out of our way. We circled around the mark boat and headed out on course chasing after *Safari* and *Yankee Girl* which had disappeared into the fog while we did our circle.

In seconds we were alone in the ocean, trapped within the frosting in our moving brandy snifter. We picked our way through the shadowy forms as they appeared ahead, trying to avoid the bad air, and after about an hour we were safely ahead of all but *Yankee Girl* and Paul Adams' *Safari* which we couldn't see but whose wind shadow's we could feel from time to time. *La Forza* would straighten up and seem to stumble in her stride— her wool telltales flickering aimlessly for a second or two and her masthead Windex revolving in lazy circles.

Later Norm spotted *Yankee Girl* ahead and to leeward in a brief partial lifting of the fog. On the midnight-to-four watch, we almost ran down her stern light (we could only assume it was *Girl,* but that was the logical explanation). We would charge up on it not realizing how close we were, and then it would be suddenly blanked out by the fog. Norm's son, Bruce, and I took turns trying to pass to windward of the night phantom. We almost got by —barely half a boatlength to windward—but the other yacht was able to parry our thrusts and stay ahead.

After dropping two boatlengths behind—almost out of sight in the fog—we tried slipping away to leeward. Our tactic appeared to work. Perhaps we had been unseen, but at least *Yankee Girl* was playing by the letter of the rules. She did not fall down on top of us as we pulled abeam and then disappeared to leeward in the fog.

A moment later a lucky header put her in our wake. We knew, under the prevailing conditions, we could fly away once our wind was undisturbed.

During the next watch Norm reported crossing *Safari*. We were alone in the lead barely twelve hours after the start.

La Forza romps on the wind in light going. That first night we had enough wind to put in the flattening reef a couple of times, but thereafter it was either medium or light number-one genoa and full main almost all the way to Halifax. I have never sailed a boat which has such an uncanny ability to make her own breeze going to windward. My own *Teazer,* back in 1967, could do it upwind but she was only twenty-four feet. *La Forza* manages it on a grand scale exceeded in modern offshore racers only by the seventy-three-foot *Kioloa.*

Time after time on *La Forza* we would watch the wind speed build past five knots, to seven, eight . . . and the speedometer would creep up from four to five to six. Meanwhile, a look at the sea (what little of it we could see) would confirm that there was less than five knots of true wind rippling the surface. Each helmsman would coax the maximum out of her until we would fly along as if on ice skates, gliding effortlessly, noiselessly, with no apparent motive force. No one else out there could be going as fast.

And no one was!

Our strategy was simple: take the shortest tack to-

Record Passage In Reverse

ward Halifax until a header or our position made the other tack favored. We seemed to ride a thumb-line draft —as we'd get to the north, we'd be headed then tack ride the lift until well south of the rhumb line and a southerly header would signal a tack back toward the north. Seeing nothing, hearing only an occasional horn or machinery noises of passing commercial craft, we sailed slowly—yet relatively, so fleetingly—toward Halifax.

The finish was frustrating; twenty miles out the wind died altogether. Even *La Forza* could not manufacture wind from nothing. We finally drifted across the finish after almost three days. It was a record slow passage, but an outstanding victory for *La Forza del Destino* on her last race under Raben's command, first to finish, first in class, and first in fleet.

It was a race of negative records: the slowest passage in the history of the Marblehead-Halifax Race; the farthest and the longest time any of us had ever sailed in total, bone-chilling fog; surely one of the very few races over three hundred miles in length that have been sailed upwind with nothing in the foretriangle smaller than a number-one genoa (not counting the drifter); and I guess it's not a record to be particularly proud of, but Jack Harvey and I landed at Kennedy International airport in New York before the second yacht—*Yankee Girl*—had finished. The last an indication of *La Forza del Destino* doing what she was designed to do exceedingly well.

VI

The Bermuda Races

CONJURING UP ALL SORTS OF images to sailor and nonsailor alike, the Bermuda Race is probably the most famous ocean race in the world. The difficulty of finding a twenty-mile-long island in midocean and the challenge of crossing a frequently storm-tossed Gulf Stream fires the imagination of all who hear about it.

I looked forward with great anticipation to my first Bermuda Race in 1960. I was going to Bermuda at last. My credentials as an ocean racer, having received their first stamp of approval almost ten years before, were about to become impeccable. When you had done a Bermuda Race, you had arrived.

The Cruising Club of America (CCA), which co-sponsors the Bermuda Race along with the Royal Bermuda Yacht Club (RBYC), uphold their race's prestigious image. They insist that two people aboard each yacht must have sailed in the race before. It is not easy to get a berth if you haven't done it previously. The sponsors also limit the total number of entries to two hundred yachts. The RBYC facilities are severely overtaxed with more than that number. This combination of requirements makes it awfully tough for a neophyte to get a berth.

It is because the race has such a prestigious reputation that these restrictions are necessary. Every damn

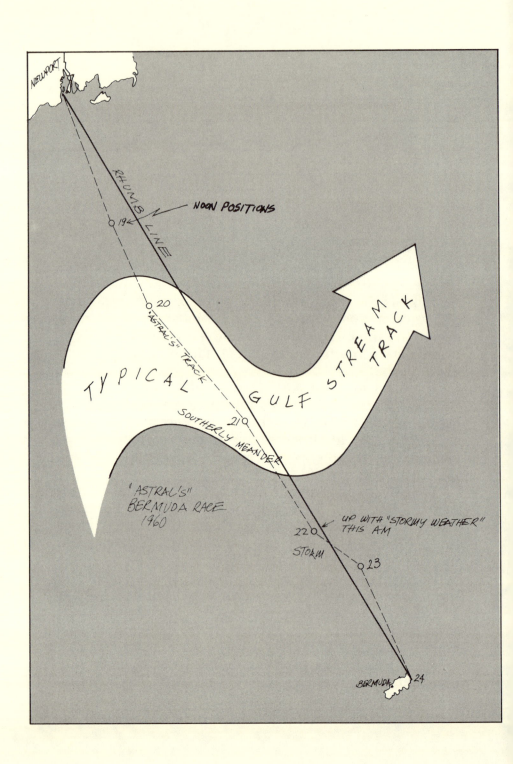

The Bermuda Races

fool with a boat would enter the race—capable or not—if the CCA and RBYC would let him. Thus, it is a self-sustaining fire that burns in the hearts of offshore racers. Because it is tough to get an invitation, more people want to go. Because more people want to go, it becomes tougher to get an invitation.

When I was working as a yacht broker with yacht designer Bill Tripp, I sold a new thirty-eight-foot Javelin to George and Howard Johnson. They wanted to race it to Bermuda in 1960, and since it would be the first Javelin to be raced, our company was anxious to provide whatever assistance we could muster for the Johnsons. Howard, a banker—not related to the restauranteur—was to be the skipper, and he asked me to sail with them as one of the watch captains. Since I had been trying to get to Bermuda since I was sixteen (when my Uncle Jack navigated the last-place Alden schooner *Sunbeam*) and I was approaching twice that age, I quickly signed on. Howard was a super organizer, and we started serious plans for the Bermuda Race a full nine months in advance.

It was the most thoroughly planned ocean race I have ever been involved with except, perhaps, for the Transatlantic Race. Crew prospects were interviewed, and final selections made. Each time a new prospect was considered, all those previously chosen were brought into the decision-making process until we had chosen a total of eight capable and compatible shipmates. Crew meetings were held every month at one of our homes, and various areas of responsibility were assigned. One of us would plan the food, one safety, another navigation and strategy, and so forth, and we would discuss where we were in various departments at each monthly meeting. Thus, every possibility was covered, every event that could be foreseen was talked over and planned for. We knew what everybody liked to eat—and didn't like. We had contingencies for coping with everything from severe hull damage to broken bones. Virtually nothing was left to chance.

The Bermuda Races

Only one problem presented itself as the March delivery date of the Johnson's Javelin came and went. We had no boat.

After relaying the vague promises of Seafarer Yachts, the importer, to the Johnsons, we got more and more nervous as race time approached. April came, and Seafarer's Brian Acworth finally admitted that the Johnson's boat had not even been started. (It was eventually delivered, almost two years late.) Now we had a crew, an organization, an *esprit de corps* built up over a winter's planning, an invitation for the Bermuda Race, but nothing to sail to Bermuda on. Hastily arranged and embarrassing meetings with the Johnsons in our offices provided the solution. Howard, George, and Al Kappel—a friend of Howard's who had signed on as one of our crew—would charter Admiral Fred Trappnel's Block Island 40 *Astral*. We were back in business.

Astral was, if anything, an improvement over the Javelin. While the latter turned out to be one of Tripp's best designs, none of the Javelins proved to be ready for sea voyages as demanding as the Bermuda Race as they came "out of the box." With *Astral* we had a proven design, and a well-shaken-down yacht with few bugs to sort out. Even so, we spent a considerable amount of time making *Astral* ready for sea. As part of the charter, Admiral Trappnel gave *Astral* to us for the major Long Island Sound races which preceed the Bermuda Race, and we attained creditable performances. By the time we set sail for Bermuda we were completely prepared, we knew our boat thoroughly, we had the confidence and ability to win the race, and our yacht was sound, fully found, and capable of winning. If people had known the extent of our preparations, and had the Johnson brothers been better known in offshore racing circles, we would surely have been one of the favorites to win. As it was, we were just another of 144 entries (135 actually started). Even we looked upon our chances as unlikely. We thought of *As-*

tral as a "dark horse" favorite. We knew we weren't supposed to do it, but we knew we could.

My personal feelings as we motored the few miles from our dock in Jamestown out to the start at Brenton Reef lightship were of quiet confidence. I knew, and I knew my shipmates knew, that we had done everything possible to prepare for the race. Mentally I surveyed all the preparations that had been made and realized that all the long checklists had been completed. There was nothing to do but stand on the foredeck as *Astral* lifted gently to the swells rolling in from Rhode Island Sound, and enjoy the feeling of quiet exhilaration that came with the realization that I was finally on my way to *Bermuda.* That long-sought goal was within my grasp.

Standing there, I noticed a piece of twine had wrapped itself around the headstay. I unsheathed my rigging knife, grasped the end of the twine with my index finger and thumb and stretched it out. With a swift, deft motion, I sliced the twine close alongside the stay, and made a neat incision near the tip of the third finger of my left hand which I had carelessly failed to retract from the path of the knife. "Damn! What a time to cut myself", I thought. Fortunately, it was not serious, and a bandaid made me almost as good as new. I had been searching in vain for a flaw—now I had one. I was to be the starting helmsman, and as we joined the milling fleet in the vicinity of the starting line I soon forgot about the finger.

Fog had been threatening since early morning, and as starting time approached it came in thick and wet. We couldn't see either end of the line from the middle. We reckoned that the lightship end was closer to Bermuda than the 325-foot Coast Guard cutter that marked the other end, and we were so close we almost didn't make it around the lightship as we started. Within minutes we were completely enveloped by fog, and while we could hear and "feel" our competitors around us, we could see nothing. But the race had begun. Bermuda, next stop.

The wind was light from the sou'west which allowed us to just lay our heading, calculated to intercept the Gulf Stream—one hundred twenty miles away—about twenty-five miles west of the rhumb-line course.

We soon settled into the routine of the ship in the pleasant (though still foggy) weather. Our watches were set—Walt Fink and Al Kapel with me in the port watch, Bob Polhemus and George Johnson with Barney Compton in the starboard watch. (Skipper, Howard Johnson, and navigator-sailing master, Buzz Knowlton did not stand regular watches but were available to each watch to avoid disturbing the off-watch for sail changes and other activities requiring more than three hands.)

The fog lifted during the night to reveal many sets of running lights all around. It was like sailing along in the middle of a moving city. By sunup there were only a few sails in sight, and we strained to identify as many as we could. Most were larger, to our gratification; we were either doing well—with our class mostly behind us—or all in our vicinity were doing poorly. We chose to believe the former, and our spirits rose. "Come on *Astral*, show them your stuff!"

Unfortunately, the light winds gradually gave way to even lighter air and then none. Daylight the second day found us in the middle of a glassy-smooth sea making almost no way. We'd drop empty beer cans over the side (after punching a hole or two in the bottom) and watch them slowly sink into the unfathomable depths. It was incredible that we were making so little way that the cans remained in sight for many seconds. The sun glinting from them as they twisted down through the clear water. Also incredible to us was the fantastic clarity of the water. It seemed you could see for thirty or fourty feet before the beer cans disappeared in the darkness below. It was as if we were in the middle of a giant millpond, sitting absolutely motionless on the glassy surface of the water. Never since, in many thousands of miles of ocean

The author counts the dots and dashes from the Nantucket Consolan transmitter aided by the beat of his pencil. Consolan, an inexpensive radio bearing system requiring only a radio receiver, was discontinued during the sixties.

sailing, have I seen the open sea so smooth—even the normally ever-present groundswell was missing.

In the evening the breeze would come back, and we would make headway under sail again. First it would be fitful cat's-paws which we'd try to snare with a light drifter. Then, when the breeze settled in, we'd set the number-one genoa, and if the wind came on with any authority we'd change down to the number two. Mostly, though, it was light close reaching with the number-one set or when the wind would come aft we'd be able to set the mizzen staysail and the spinnaker.

Early in the night of the second day, a set of running lights appeared from our leeward quarter and passed close aboard to disappear in the night toward the west. It was *Finnesterre,* Carlton Mitchell's Nevins 40 yawl. This was a good sign. *Finnesterre* had won the two previous races, and she was in our class. We were in good company. Not ahead yet, but we could be! If our course was correct, we'd soon be many miles ahead.

One day was much like the next. We felt good. While it was hot and frustrating both below and on deck, we felt we were doing well—continuing on our high from being surrounded by larger boats and seeing *Finnisterre*—and we were getting closer and closer to Bermuda.

In spite of the lack of wind, Buzz's navigation indicated that we were making good progress. We had no way of knowing for sure but the Gulf Stream was apparently bent in a "meander" toward the south. We had hit it just right, and the three- to four-knot current whisked us toward our goal while we sat, often motionless, on the surface.

Walt, Al, and I were on watch the morning of the fourth day. It had been a quiet night—as all so far had been—and the morning breeze was blowing faintly from the south-southwest. Walt was on the helm, and he was doing wonders with *Astral,* coaxing every available ounce of drive out of the zephyrs. The early morning sky

The Bermuda Races

was cloudy but there was excellent visibility. As the light increased it revealed one sail after another. Soon I could see boats all around—and at one point I counted eighty-eight sails.

We normally changed helmsmen every half-hour to keep from growing stale, but Walt had done so well during his trick that I asked him to keep at it—not wanting to lose the momentum that he had built up. He stayed at the wheel for three hours, coaxing *Astral* along in the calm, and during that time we moved from the back of that eighty-eight-boat pack to the front. Incredibly, we found ourselves in company with boats like the sixty-eight-foot *Cotton Blossom.* Every sail we could identify belonged to a yacht in a class larger than ours. With only one hundred twenty miles to go, we were pinching ourselves in disbelief over our good fortune. We were winning the Bermuda race!

We turned *Astral* over to Barney's watch after lunch and settled in for a long afternoon nap. The wind came up gradually, and by mid-afternoon Barney called us out to tuck in a reef, our first of the race, and an hour later we were called out again. By the time we took over again after supper it was piping up to half a gale.

Soon the seas were crested with whitecaps which blew off the tops and shattered against the back of our oilskins. We were down to the working jib and mizzen, and Barney's watch had set the storm trysail, after taking down the mainsail, to give *Astral* better balance and provide more drive than we could get from jib and mizzen alone. We were on port tack as the wind had backed—blowing now almost directly from Bermuda. Al was at the helm.

The wind continued to increase, screaming as it blew through the rigging. *Astral* heeled menacingly with each blast, and Al—thinking it best to ease the pressure—allowed her to come up closer to the wind. When he did so, the jib would luff, shaking as if to tear itself to pieces, setting up an incredible din as its flailing leach slapped in the wind, and sending its vibrations down through the spars and the headstay to rattle every glass fiber in *Astral*'s stout hull. Unknown to us on deck, Buzz, Howard, and Barney were holding a council of war. The sensations down there in *Astral*'s cabin must have been terrifying as she crashed from wave to wave, shuddered and shook luffing in the gusts. Howard's ashen face appeared in the companionway. "Heave her to," he commanded, and it was clear that this was not open to discussion—as all our previous decisions had been—this was an absolute order from our captain.

Discouraged though I was I did not argue. I thought we could still sail, and it turned out that Barney and Buzz shared my opinion. Howard was the captain, however, and the made it clear he would stand for no delay in carrying out this order. Buzz came on deck to help me take in the working jib, and as we cast off the halyard a tremendous blast caught *Astral* full aback. She laid over on the starboard tack, her jib, now loose, flailing on the stay. Buzz, who had been moving forward to help me pull down the jib, was flipped over the lifelines. He did a complete somersault over the upper line, through the lower, and ended up hanging by his knees over the rail—his body completely out of the boat. Standing with my back to the bow pulpit, my feet went out from under me and I fetched up dangling by my armpits from the pulpit, my feet out of the boat into the sea.

Both of us were attached to *Astral* with safety harnesses, but it was an eerie sight to see Buzz pulling himself up over the gunwhale as I struggled to hoist my feet back up to the relative security of the heaving deck. In due course we got the jib down, the halyard stowed, the hanks unclipped, and the jib passed below; but it was exhausting work, clinging to the lifelines with one hand as the bouncing bow threatened to pitch us into the dark, frothing sea, trying to catch an elusive jib hank with the other hand and unclip it without letting it get away.

The Bermuda Races

When it was done, Buzz went below and I sat on the weather deck, clinging to the lifelines, fighting off the nauseous fatigue that numbed my body.

Soon Howard beckoned for me to go below, and he explained the reasons for his decision. George was seasick, the rest of the crew who had been up all afternoon fighting to keep *Astral* at her peak were exhausted. He himself did not feel well—which was obvious from his pale, drawn face. It was not his yacht, but Admiral Trappnel's, which we were sailing into jeopardy, and he did not want the responsibility of continuing to race in conditions in which we could well lose both yacht and crew. (Later, he confessed that he knew that *Astral* was underinsured, and that he and Al had guaranteed to indemnify the admiral from any loss not covered.) It was decided to set two-man, two-hour watches with the helm lashed to minimize headway. Walt and I took the first two-hour trick after I had put on dry longjohns under my foul-weather gear, (a very good warm-weather combination, I found) and *Astral* lay reasonably comfortably with the storm trysail sheeted to the weather quarter (we had not had to touch the sheet after our sudden tack) and the helm lashed hard over to starboard.

Sitting on deck in the raging fury, my main concern was that we should come upon another boat and be unable to maneuver away from a collision. We could see scores of lights—red, green, and white—bouncing close by in the waves. It was eerie—even frightening—seeing the evidence of other yachts but being powerless to avoid them, wondering how they were managing in the storm. *Astral* seemed quite capable of fending for herself against the elements, but a collision in those conditions would have been disastrous.

Unbeknownst to us, somewhere not far away a man aboard a sister Block Island 40 was thrown out of the companionway and into the sea as he tried to make his way below. Miraculously, he was rescued by his shipmates after he had spent over an hour in the raging sea

—the first documented rescue attributed to the then-new xenon strobe waterlight which his shipmates had thrown to him. Also, not far away, two yachts were dismasted, others, including *Cotton Blossom,* lost rudders, and eight crewmen who had been sitting to windward suddenly found themselves up to their armpits in water as the wind-shift that put us aback put their yacht about and buried what had been her windward rail into the water. Later reports put the wind velocity at eighty knots, the most violent storm ever to hit a Bermuda race fleet.

I slept like a baby despite the raging storm when Walt and I were relieved from our watch. We had not come any closer to the other bouncing lights, and gradually they had all disappeared, leaving us alone in the tossing storm. The next thing I knew, it was light. The motion was still violent, but as I poked my head through the companionway it was obvious that the wind had abated considerably. Walt and George were on deck, and I donned my oilskins and joined them.

"Let's make sail", I said to Walt, and I climbed past him to hoist the mizzen. Even getting that small sail up was a substantial effort, and when I had finished I sat panting on the deck. The seas were wild. There seemed to be two components to their direction, and *Astral* responded with a crazy, unpredictable motion with insufficient sail up to steady her in the wind.

After a breather, I took the jib forward and tried to hank it on. The effort, again, was almost more than I could muster, and it seemed to take me hours to do a job that in smooth water would have taken me only a minute. Finally I got the job done, struggled aft to the mast and hoisted the sail. *Astral* came alive as Walt and George got the sail sheeted in. We were once again on our way to Bermuda, but in the twenty-four hours since our triumphal drift to the head of the pack, we had made only fifty-six miles. I slumped against the cabin side on the windward deck on the verge of throwing up from the

The protracted calm before the storm. Walter Fink tries in vain to coax *Astral* to life while the author splices an afterguy—something to do while waiting for a breeze.

combination of the motion and the exhausting effort, but I was saved by an ice-cold orange thrust through the companionway by Barney. Never has an orange tasted so good, and its sugar soon had me feeling well again.

Our watch system was blown. Our position was uncertain. Our elation of the day before was squashed. We discussed our chances—fooling ourselves that no one could have sailed through that storm—thinking we'd still be okay.

Walt and George retired to the forward cabin to get some rest when Al and Bob came on deck, and I took the helm. For quite a while I guided *Astral* through the confused seas, snaking her around the crests which occasionally would peak to astounding heights as the two wave patterns met. *Astral* was sailing well, taking the seas in her stride, and at one point I just got lazy and decided to let her have her head.

We met one of the monster peaks which reared up as the two wave systems came together. Instead of guiding her around, I let *Astral*'s bow climb up the face of the wave. She shot off the top, and to my horror I could see that there was a yawning abyss on the other side. Too late. *Astral*'s bow hurtled into the air, and when the wave passed under her center of buoyancy, her bow smashed down about fifteen feet into the trough below. Transfixed, I clung to the wheel and watched the mast buckle forward as we hit. I was sure it would collapse, breaking the lower shrouds with the strain, but while it appeared to jerk forward a full two feet, the mast held, and *Astral* shook the water from her decks and resumed sailing.

Walt and George, in the forward cabin, felt the world drop out from under them, and then an instant later they were smashed into the bunks and each other amid sails, drawers, and other debris lifted out of its stowage. How they survived without injury I don't know, but a minute later Walt appeared at the hatch. "What was *that?*" he asked, looking thoroughly shaken. Thereafter I was more careful where I steered.

Our arrival in Bermuda was less than triumphant. The wind and seas gradually abated, and the final seventy miles was pleasant enough except that we were a thoroughly disheartened crew. Bermuda Radio broadcasted the arrival of one after another of our competitors. *Finnisterre* was declared the winner, for an unprecedented three-in-a-row, before we even had Bermuda in sight. We were not last, but we certainly weren't first.

Perhaps because of our rapid decline, perhaps for other, unrelated reasons, our closely knit crew fell apart once we had reached shore. We moored *Astral* in front of Al Kappel's house, "Fleetwood," on Spithead in Paget (Al's wife Vicki was the sister of a former governor of Bermuda, and the Kappels maintained a home there), a more idyllic setting you couldn't imagine. But the wives and friends had been there for days, wondering when we would be in, and straining to be civil to each other in unfamiliar surroundings. Soon we split into "armed" camps each accusing the other of some foul transgression or another. It was a tough several hours until Al came to the rescue. "You are now *my* guests in *my* home," he told us, "we are no longer at sea. Please relax and enjoy yourselves."

From that point on we did as he suggested, placing ourselves in the hands of our gracious host and hostess. Still, the close friendships—the camaraderie—that we had developed over the past nine months was strained beyond repair. While we remained friends, the closeness we had shared as a crew was gone, never to be recaptured.

TO BERMUDA AGAIN

Now that I had finally made a Bermuda race, I naturally wanted to keep the string going. It didn't look good, in 1962, for a repeat as I had left the brokerage firm and was

Astral at anchor off "Fleetwood Manor" looking none the worse for her rough passage to Bermuda.

working at a temporary job as a rigger at Minneford's Yacht Yard—where many of the top yachts of the day were stored and fitted out. Race day approached, and I not only didn't have a berth, I made no effort to secure one.

A few days before the race, Barney Compton called and asked me if I'd go. He was sailing with J. Carter Brown aboard John Nicholas Brown's Block Island 40 *Volta.* One of their crew had backed out at the last minute, and Barney had suggested that I replace him. Much to the consternation of an old-timer with whom I worked at Minneford's ("What do you want to go and do a thing like that for, Sonny?"), I got leave from the yard foreman to take the week off. I stepped directly from the bosom of the working-class former professional seaman who were my companions at Minneford's into Newport's opulence at the magnificant "summer cottage" called "Harbor Court"—the senior Brown's home overlooking the Ida Lewis Yacht Club anchorage. Mrs. Brown graciously apologized that I had to sleep in the third-floor "children's wing," but I pointed out that the following night I would be bunked down in a crowded sailboat in the Atlantic Ocean.

In the morning we had a civilized breakfast looking out over the expansive lawn at *Volta* bobbing patiently at her mooring, waiting for us to take her to sea.

There was nothing unusual or noteworthy about the 1962 Bermuda Race. It was a reach all the way on starboard tack (as it often is) and we used only the number-one genoa, or reacher. Once or twice the wind came far enough aft for a spinnaker, and we carried on an endless debate as to whether the mizzen staysail would help or not. We sailed well, we had thought, went the right way (was there any choice?), and came in at the middle of the fleet.

It was wonderful sailing with no storms, no calms, hot days, and cool nights. The Gulf Stream, usually squally and rough, was hardly discernible. All told it was a bit boring.

Our navigator was a young friend of Carter's who was doing his first Bermuda Race. He had obtained a new set of contact lenses especially for the trip, and each time he would come on deck with his sextant to take a sun line or an evening star, his eyes would continually blink from the unaccustomed irritation of the contacts. "Blinky," as Barney nicknamed him, did not inspire us with confidence. Ordinarily, on a passage of six hundred miles with a destination only twenty miles long, one would worry about questionable navigation. However, we were never out of sight of fewer than four or five competitors, so we doubters weren't really worried. One learns to take certain things on faith. In fact, Blinky's landfall was right on.

In contrast to our stay at the Kappel's two years previously, this adventure in Bermuda was quite different. We had no large house with beds, showers, servants, prepared meals, and open bar as at Fleetwood. Instead, we stayed aboard *Volta,* anchored off the RBYC and stood in line for cold showers in the clubhouse. It was different, but still fun.

The day we were to leave, Barney returned in midmorning with an opened bottle of Teddy Gosling's "Old Barbados" rum. Bob Polhemus (who had sailed down with someone else and was flying home with us) came with him. "Got to finish this before we leave," said Barney, pouring rum into coffee cups in *Volta*'s galley, "can't take this with us if it's been opened."

A "regular" crew member aboard Bill Snaith's *Figaro,* (I'll call him "Smitty") had moved aboard *Volta,* and as Barney passed out the run he persuaded Smitty to tell us an incredible tale of *Figaro*'s cook in an ocean race a few years previously. The crew had taken an oath of secrecy, but oiled with Old Barbados, Smitty told.

Bill Snaith was something of a gourmet, and often planned and prepared the meals aboard *Figaro* as well as acting as her skipper. However, for long races, as a transatlantic surely is, he preferred to have someone aboard

The Bermuda Races

whose specific duty was cooking and galley maintenance. At the last minute *Figaro*'s cook had been forced to cancel, so Snaith signed on a "pier-head jumper" who swore that he was an experienced offshore hand and cook.

"Cooky" as we shall call him had, in fact, never been to sea on a sailboat. The first night when Snaith asked him to go below to prepare dinner (a good cook shouldn't need to be told when to get to work, according to Smitty), he stalled and hesitated. When Snaith pressed him with a "... get your ass below and cook goddammit, that's what you signed on to do," Cooky replied weakly, "I can't, its too rough."

"Snaith couldn't persuade him," Smitty told us—warming to both his subject and the rum—"and he put 'Cooky' on one of the watches and told us we'd have to rotate the galley chores." The meals had all been planned by Snaith and packed, complete with instructions, meal by meal in special stowage by Betty Snaith, so the crew wouldn't starve or be forced to a steady diet of Dinty Moore's beef stew.

Cooky proved to be as bad a shipmate as he was a cook. He was continually late for his watch. After an all-hands call to reef, his watch mates would return below soaking in their underwear to find Cooky pulling on his boots and foul-weather gear—the job on deck having been done without him. During a squall he was sent forward to help douse the genoa, but he got only as far as the mainmast which he clung to like grim death. He was worse than useless as a crew member—even managing to plug the toilet which he then refused to clean up.

Barney kept the rum flowing, and Smitty kept the stories coming. They spewed out of him—having been bottled up inside for years—as he warmed to his subject.

Snaith's crew was both closely knit and tough. It would be hard enough for an outsider to gain their trust and confidence, but this character was absolutely impossible. Ashore, one can get away from people who are unpleasant or irritating, and have no further contact with them. On board a small boat in the middle of the ocean, personal relationships are difficult among the best of friends, and everyone has to work hard—be especially tolerant and considerate—to avoid friction. Cooky couldn't be ignored or avoided, he was always in the way, he wouldn't help, he couldn't do anything, he was surly, and he whined continually. "We all grew to hate him," Smitty told us. "I mean real *hate.*" The rum sloshed out of his cup as he pounded it on the galley counter for emphasis. One crew member openly threatened to kill Cooky if he ever got in his way. Another told him in all seriousness, "Don't you ever get between me and the rail."

I was appalled that people I knew would actually consider what Smitty told us they had threatened, yet I could understand the depth of emotion that could exist under the circumstances. How easy it would be to casually bump someone you hated over the side on a dark, stormy night. Under the circumstances, your shipmates would never accuse you, even if they suspected the truth. In fact, years later on another ship, an acquaintance of mine may have met just such a fate. He "fell" overboard and was never found.

No one did Cooky in, fortunately, but for him it must have been a terrifying three weeks. Imagine discovering after it is too late that the sea is rougher and more vast than you had ever expected. Imagine the gut-twisting fear augmented by the knowledge that everyone in your small world—from which there is no escape—hates you and that some of them say they hate you enough to kill you. We sat spellbound as Smitty's story concluded.

When they got to their destination, Snaith ordered Cooky off the boat. "But I have no place to go," he whined, "I don't have enough money to get home."

"Snaith told him 'Tough shit,' " Smitty said, " 'I'll give you five minutes to pack your gear and get off my boat' and as he [Cooky] moved through the cabin we all lined up and hit him with our fists. I guess we weren't very proud of that—any of us—but we did it. I don't know where he went, but we never saw him again."

"I know where he went," I said drunkenly—it was almost lunchtime and the rum bottle was empty, "He came to me and tried to buy his own sailboat." Why, unless he had to prove something to himself, I found hard to understand.

By the time Smitty had finished his story we were all quite drunk. Somehow we each assembled our gear and got ashore. Though we were sobering up as we rode in a taxi from Hamilton to the airport near Saint George's—half the length of the island away, I thought Barney and Bob were behaving outrageously, and I warned them that if the stewardess on the airplane thought we were drunk she wouldn't serve us any more drinks. The thought of a two-hour flight back to New York in a sobering condition was more than we could bear.

We boarded our flight, which taxied out to the runway and then returned to the ramp—engine trouble. They would feed us in the airport restaurant, but that didn't include alcoholic beverages, and there were none available at the airport. We pooled our remaining resources, and Barney took a taxi to Tom Moore's restaurant a few miles away and soon returned with three glasses of rum. The plane was fixed, and we reboarded with just enough money left for one round of drinks. Happily, the airline served free drinks, as a sop for our delayed departure, and we flew drunkenly back to New York singing and laughing, and when the plane landed everybody cheered.

Bob took one of our last dimes and called his wife in Noroton, Connecticut. Pat agreed to come pick us up—as we didn't have enough money left for a limousine—and we sobered up slowly and painfully, sitting on our duffle bags for the two hours it took her to round up a babysitter and drive to Idlewild.

Now I had two Bermuda Races in my ocean-racing résumé, and a story I couldn't tell—until now.

THE 1964 BERMUDA RACE

Two of our customers at Tripp & Campbell who became good friends were George Moffett and Humphrey Simson. Both had bought Bermuda 40s, Bill Tripp's successor design to the Block Island 40, and I had sailed with both. George raced in the SORC in 1962 and then raced a 5.5-Meter in a special series in Nassau following the Circuit. I had sailed the Miami-Nassau race with him and then crewed for him the following week in the 5.5-Meter. This followed the collapse of the Tripp-Campbell partnership, just before I took my temporary job at Minneford's.

Alan Gurney had come to work for Tripp about a year before. Both George and Humphrey got to know Alan, recognized his talent, and became his friends and first customers when he went out on his own. Alan's first design—after an aborted 5.5-Meter for Moffett—was the Nantucket 38, which George commissioned to be built of wood in Denmark. The "Bucket 38" as we referred to this second *Guinevere* (the name for all of Moffett's ocean racers) started her career in the spring of '64, and I was one of her regular crew members.

This *Guinevere* was beautifully built and had many design innovations. Unfortunately, she was not one of Alan's fastest designs. She went well upwind and downwind, but for reasons I could never understand, she wouldn't reach worth a damn. However, she was comfortable, and we had fun racing her. "Hump" Simson's Bermuda 40 was our great rival, and since I had sailed many times with him, I was always as anxious as anyone that we beat him. Not only that, but my wife was sailing on *Kittiwake* in her first Bermuda race—a "must win" situation for me if I was to avoid an endless ribbing from our friends.

In the spring races we found that *Guinevere* was a bit faster than *Kittiwake* but we also rated slightly higher. All our races were close, and we felt that we had a better

The Bermuda Races

than even chance against them going to Bermuda.

This was to be my first race to Bermuda without Barney Compton as a shipmate, but he was aboard *Kittiwake,* adding further spice to the competition. It was very serious, in a friendly way, but not very intense. We'd tie up together before and after the early spring races, trying to psyche each other before and making boasts or excuses (as appropriate) afterwards. It was good sport.

The Bermuda Race in '64 was a carbon copy of the one in '62. Pleasant sailing on a close reach all the way. Although it was not *Guinevere*'s race, it was delightful sailing for most of us. It was the first crew I had sailed with in which chronic seasickness was a problem. Two of our younger, less experienced crew members were out of commission for the first two days, and the navigator was sick the whole time. The weather wasn't at all rough, but the ocean rollers—hour after hour—get to some people. Others it never bothers.

I never understood why anyone would go to sea in a small sailboat knowing in advance that he would be ill. Many people get over it in a couple of days, as most of our crew did, but there are those few—like our navigator (I will call him "Fred")—who are invariably ill and stay that way until they get ashore.

Fred developed a routine to deal with his sickness, and he was, in fact, a very accurate navigator. He would appear on deck for his sights, then he'd go below, work them up, plot our position, and then turn into his bunk. We'd wake him up (at his request) in time for him to get the next sight. Fred would cram a handful of saltines into his bearded face, and repeat the sight-taking and reduction process. Frequently he would appear on deck after working out our position, sitting on the leeward cockpit seat with his back to the cabin. After a while, Fred would lean over the rail, heave up what was left of the saltines, wipe his beard with a paper towel and disappear below to his bunk until it was time for the next sight. What an existence! I could never put up with that sort of problem, even for all the joys of ocean sailing. Many times, for much less reason, I have thought to myself that if I were ever lucky enough to get ashore I would never go to sea again—but those memories pass, and you always eagerly volunteer the next time you are called. But chronic seasickness like Fred's would not be so easily forgotten. I couldn't do it. While I would prefer not to sail with someone like Fred, I had to admire his courage and his ability to rise above his affliction.

We had last seen *Kittiwake* falling far behind us soon after the start of the race, but after four days of relatively dull reaching we converged with her as we approached the Northeast Breaker buoy a few miles from the finish line. The Northeast Breaker buoy is usually the first marker to be encountered as you approach Bermuda. From there you must pass Kitchen Shoals to starboard and a number of lesser buoys marking the reef from Kitchen Shoals to the finish off Diamond Heat lighthouse. From Northeast Breaker to Kitchen Shoals it was a beat favoring the starboard tack followed by a shorter port tack favored beat to the finish. The sight of *Kittiwake* just ahead was not a happy one, but it gave us something to spice up the race—we must catch and pass her before the finish.

Naturally, they spotted us and were just as anxious to beat us as we were to beat them. Both crews came to life, everyone was on deck and onto the weather rail. We trimmed sails with a will that had gradually diminished over the previous days of dull reaching. Slowly we closed the gap, and at the tack just after passing Kitchen Shoals we were able to get ahead. However, struggle as we might, there was no way we could put enough time between us to save our time on *Kittiwake*. We, at least, had the satisfaction of beating them boat for boat, but they beat us on handicap. I suppose it was a just climax to our friendly rivalry.

Barney Compton at the helm of *Astral* in 1960 just before the storm. The author and Compton sailed together on several Bermuda Races, Transatlantic (Chapter VII), Saint Petersburg to Fort Lauderdale (Chapter XI), and others, as well as spending a day together aground under the Triborough Bridge (Chapter II)

On the long run under power from Saint George's to Hamilton, *Guinevere* and *Kittiwake* moved side by side —her crews swapping insults, sea stories, and trying to drench each other with buckets of water. It was a fun way to end a race.

When the results were tallied, *Kittiwake* was scored next to last in our class, and *Guinevere* was last. Once again, my ship had not distinguished itself in a Bermuda Race. Once again, I had finished in the middle of the fleet —which is much better than saying "last in class." I was beginning to think that I did not have the key to success going to Bermuda.

NUMBER FOUR IN THE STRING

In 1965 both George Moffett and Humphrey Simson commissioned Alan Gurney to design new boats for them. George's third *Guinevere* and Humphrey's third *Kittiwake* were respectively forty-eight and forty-seven feet overall. *Kittiwake* was launched first, and I sailed that first season exclusively with Hump, a more easygoing and considerate skipper you couldn't imagine. *Kittiwake*'s first series was Block Island Week, and Hump loaned her to me a few weeks later for the American Yacht Club Cruise in part so Alan could show off his latest creation to other potential design customers. We did well—she was spectacularly fast offwind in light going (and as we learned later, upwind in a gale)—and after the cruise I thanked Humphrey by grounding his new yacht hard trying to pass through Robinson's Hole in the Elizabeth Islands. A true gentleman, Hump said not to worry, and then he grounded her himself a few weeks later off Block Island. He told me he couldn't tell his dent from mine when he had *Kittiwake* hauled.

Humphrey planned to do the 1966 Transatlantic Race from Bermuda to Denmark, and I signed on to do the SORC that winter—which we would use for preparing *Kittiwake* for our long sea voyage and to try out prospective crew members. Hump was both skipper and navigator while I had the starboard watch and Barney had the port.

At some point during the Circuit, we discovered that we could keep Humphrey off the helm in certain critical situations when we thought someone else could handle it better, and after the Miami-Nassau Race we realized that Hump hadn't touched the wheel at all. Naturally, we didn't say anything to him, but he was surely as aware of it as we. That started a rather astounding five thousand miles, plus, of ocean racing in which our skipper never steered his own boat.

I had changed jobs in '65, becoming an associate editor of *One-Design & Offshore Yachtsman* magazine, and one of the conditions I placed on accepting the position was that I be allowed time to race transatlantic with Humphrey. That wasn't too difficult a compromise for publisher Knowles Pittman to make because my primary responsibility was to be the offshore racing editor.

For one of my early articles I researched recent work that had been done by the Woods Hole Oceanographic Institute. I assembled quite a bit of information and became a pseudo-expert on the Stream as it affected the Bermuda Race. By this time the periodic meanders had been more thoroughly studied, and it became apparent why certain strategies which had been learned by trial and error over the years often proved valid. Southerly meanders, like the one we must have encountered in 1960 to push us so far with so little wind, could have such a dramatic effect on a yacht's speed over the bottom that it was absolutely essential to "guess right" to do well in this race. A couple of miles east or west could mean a difference in speed over the ocean floor of as much as five or six knots. In the right place a yacht could have three knots of current flowing almost directly on the course for Bermuda. A few miles to the east another yacht could have a two-knot current flowing in the opposite direction. It doesn't matter in these conditions how well or how poorly a yacht is sailed. The one in the right place will come out of the Stream ahead of the other. Of course, the well-sailed yacht in the right place will do very well indeed.

This phenomenon is explained in detail in *The Offshore Racer** as well as the June 1966 issue of *One-Design & Offshore Yachtsman,* † but since it is so crucially important a factor in the Bermuda race, I will cover it again briefly here.

In the area between the Florida Straits and Cape Hatteras, the Gulf Stream, which is a band of warm water spewing out of the Caribbean and the Gulf of Mexico, flows in a more or less straight line at speeds of approximately four knots. (Current velocities of from two knots south to eleven knots north have been reported.) However, from Cape Hatteras on out into the North Atlantic —cutting directly across the Bermuda racecourse—the Stream often undulates like a snake. These undulations are referred to as "meanders" and they can be up to sixty miles in length. It had always been thought that the Gulf Stream maintained its more or less straight line and as long as this theory prevailed the Bermuda race strategy was relatively simple—cross at right angles and get through as quickly as you can. This led to the development of a standard plan—try to hit the Stream twenty to forty miles west of the rhumb-line course so you come out the other side on the rhumb line. No one ever went east! However, with the discovery of the meanders, the strategy became much more complicated. Obviously, it is imperative to enter a southerly flowing meander and pick up its southerly flowing current. Just as obviously is the

---

*Theodore A. Jones, *The Offshore Racer,* Quadrangle, New York, 1973, Chapter 8.
†Ted Jones, "Beating the Gulf Stream to Bermuda." *One-Design & Offshore Yachtsman,* Chicago, June 1966 p. 11.

The Bermuda Races

converse—avoid a northerly flowing meander.

The theory is simple, but the tricks are to determine if there is a meander; if so, where is it located; and how do you tell, when you get where you thought it was, if it is really there. While there are often visual signs of the Stream's presence, it isn't like a white line painted down the middle of a road. The most precise method is to measure the temperature of the water. This, in turn, is not as simple as it would appear because the surface temperature may be affected by the sun. One wants to measure the water temperature, optimally, at a depth of sixty feet or more.

It is theoretically possible to locate a meander by turning east or west when the northern edge of the Stream has been encountered. If you turn east and move back into cold water, it is very likely that a meander is present to the west of your position. If you turn east and there is no drop in temperature there may or may not be a meander, but if there is one you are in it. If you turn west and the water temperature drops, there most likely is a meander to the east of your position. If you turn west and the water temperature rises there may or may not be a meander, but if there is you are in it—and so forth. The only difficulty with this theory is that no one wants to sail off course for any length of time. However, the alternative is to trust to luck.

There is another tool which could be used to fantastic advantage, but the Bermuda Race sponsors do not allow it. Loran—which was not very common in yachts in 1966—is a precise long-range electronic navigation system which can pinpoint a ship's position instantaneously within *yards.* If Loran could be used in the Bermuda Race to determine the effects of the Gulf Stream it would take the guesswork out of the race. As long as this tool is prohibited for use in the Stream, the Bermuda Race will be a "crap shoot."

The U.S. Coast and Geodetic Survey provided information on the Gulf Stream for the 1966 Bermuda race.

Humphrey and I went over it and plotted our strategy—a conference which must have occurred at least once for every competitor. It looked simple enough. There was a meander reported just east of the rhumb line, and virtually every yacht in the race headed for the same spot about one hundred twenty miles south-southeast of Newport.

The weather for the race was nasty, ". . . might be described as 'unpleasant' by normal people," I wrote in the race report in *O-D&OY*. Only one afternoon was spent out of foul-weather gear. The Gulf Stream was up to its more usual tricks as I had seen them off Florida but never before in a Bermuda race: squally, rough, fickle winds which required different sails to be set every few minutes. It was hard, frustrating work keeping *Kittiwake* moving at her best in these conditions which lasted for days.

Guinevere finished well, placing fourth in our class. We were okay—tenth in class and seventy-fourth in fleet. We were luckier than those who finished behind us, however. Late Wednesday evening, with approximately half the fleet still at sea, a violent storm whipped through the area just north of Bermuda, and while there was no serious damage it was a cruel blow to those who had suffered through the four days of rough weather and change upon endless change of sail. Some of them, with their goal in sight, found themselves battered by winds too high to sail against and blown away from their longed-for tropical paradise.

By comparison we were lucky indeed. *Kittiwake* was safely at anchor, and her crew was warm and dry, with firm ground under foot enjoying the luxury of wine, women, and song.

There was no returning from Bermuda this time. After a week of relaxing and taking care of some noncritical repairs, *Kittiwake,* among forty-one other starters, was off across thirty-six hundred miles of open ocean to Copenhagen. But that's another tale (see Chapter VIII).

The Bermuda Races

111

THE END OF THE STRING

With the 1966 Bermuda Race completed, I now had four in a row—a true veteran—and every intention of making it an ongoing series until I was too old to hang onto a heaving deck. I was signed on aboard *Kittiwake* again in '68, but my grandmother suffered a fatal stroke two days before the start, and I had no choice but to cancel out of the crew at the last minute. I was able to fly down a few days later to cover the story for the magazine, but it was a poor second best to having sailed. One quickly tires of answering the inevitable question, "Who did you sail down with?" "Well, I was supposed to be on *Kittiwake*, but. . . ." Still, I was glad to be in Bermuda again. It turned out to be my last visit for six years.

By 1970 I was becoming disillusioned with the merits of the Bermuda Race as a yacht race. The navigational challenge of finding the island, the physical challenge of fighting the elements will always be a part of the race, but as a test of racing skill it is a sham as long as the effects of the Gulf Stream are left largely to luck. By 1970 the cost of Loran had come down low enough to remove price as a valid objection to its use. However, the CCA and RBYC still clung to the notion that a navigator would rely so heavily in fancy electronic gadgetry that he would forget how to use his sextant. Position-finding by reference to heavenly bodies may be reliable (as long as it isn't cloudy), but it is not accurate enough or quick enough to be of any help determining the effects of current in the Stream. In 1970 I opted not to go to Bermuda. Ditto, 1972.

The day before the start of the 1972 Bermuda race found me driving to Newport, Rhode Island, on business totally unrelated to the race. About halfway along the Connecticut Turnpike past Bermuda races came into mental focus. Vivid pictures of the Gulf Stream and Bermuda sprang to mind. There was the exhilaration of tension before the start. I could actually see the incredible

The Bermuda Races

blue-green of the sea and the translucent white bow wave lifting off to leeward. I cast a suspicious eye at a passing cloud and imagined rain lashing down in sheets, turning the ocean's surface into millions of tiny volcanoes. Barney Compton clowned with a flying fish between his teeth sticking out of his grizzly beard. The "endless" beat from Kitchen Shoals buoy to the finish was finally terminated with the beautiful sight of Bermuda's pastel houses with their white roofs sparkling amid the lush green of the island's vegetation.

It was the first time I had thought about this year's Bermuda race, and with a pang of regret I wished that I could go. Circumstances—meaning bad planning, trying to do too much in too little time, the demands of others—were keeping me from something I suddenly wanted to do very badly. Damn it! I must not let this happen again.

I had been putting down the Bermuda race of late, talking about how much luck plays a part in the outcome, about how much more a racer's race it would be if Loran were allowed and how, for these reasons, the Bermuda race doesn't deserve its reputation as one of the world's most prestigious offshore races. An easy rationalization since I have never been on a boat that has done well. All wrong. It's not how well you do in the Bermuda race that counts, it's how you do it and the fact that when you've finished you've done it well and in a seamanlike manner.

There's something else: the very thing that was keeping me from going is one of the great reasons to go. When you race to Bermuda you can put aside all the niggling responsibilities that keep whittling away at your time ashore. Here is the opportunity to concentrate for three or four days on one project: racing to Bermuda. It's much different from just sailing there because the sea around you is filled with people and boats doing the same thing. You cannot slack off, take it easy. You keep driving with maximum effort to keep ahead of the competition, driving harder than the others, always with a weather eye on the clouds and the subconscious realization that, in addition to winning or losing, your survival may depend upon your skill and the skill of your shipmates. There just isn't anything as encompassing, as mind-blowing as racing to Bermuda.

When I got to Newport, it too was just as exciting as ever. Jaded with a summer full of America's Cup activity in 1970, I had avoided the place in 1971. Now in June of 1972 Newport was as bustling and unique as ever, and I realized that I loved this city as no other yachting center. Here at Port-O-Call, Christies, Newport Shipyard, Williams & Manchester, and across the harbor were all the exciting new boats to be seen, Bob Grant's C&C 61 *Robon*, Norm Raben's Gary Mull-designed *La Forza del Destino*, George Kiskaddon's John Spencer-schooner *New World*. There were the U.S. Onion Patch team yachts *Charisima, Yankee Girl*, and *Aura*; the foreign yachts *Apollo, Buccaneer, Fjord VI, Saga*, and *Noryema*; and, of course, the "monsters" *Ondine, Blackfin*, and *Windward Passage*, as well as Bill Tripp's design, *The Hawk*, at the minimum size.

Out on Thames Street in front of J. T. O'Connell's and the Armory, behind The Candy Store, inside The Pier, and all over The Black Pearl and Mac's Clam Shack was everybody you ever heard of connected with offshore racing. It was Newport at its best.

Afterwards, when one of the roughest Bermuda races was over, people said that I must be glad to have missed it. I said that I surely was, because that's the sensible and expected answer. Certainly I would have wanted to be somewhere else were I aboard *Passage* with all the sails in rags or aboard *Nepenthe* with her mast over the side, or with one of the tailenders struggling past the Northeast Breaker buoy in big seas and almost no wind. I might not have minded quite so much being aboard *Kittiwake*, but if I had, with my dismal record they probably wouldn't have finished second in class.

It would have been nice to have been there, at least to have arrived safely and to have been enjoying a planter's punch on the lawn of the Royal Bermuda Yacht Club.

AFTER A SIX YEAR HIATUS . . .

Joe McBrien, a Canadian with whom I had sailed in several SORC races, chartered one of Ted Hood's *Robin*-series One-tonners for the 1974 Bermuda race. *Robin Too* was a keel boat, somewhat lighter than Hood's centerboarders, and she had done well the previous year in the Saint Petersburg Yacht Club's match racing series. *Robin Too* was to be a member of the Canadian Onion Patch team—the trophy awarded to national teams of three yachts which score best in the Bermuda race and three preceding events—and I was honored as the only non-Canadian to be asked to sail on this team.

I had had to hedge my commitment with Joe because I could not race in any of the earlier races. It was agreed that if he needed me I would be available, but that if he felt he didn't want an eighth crew member I would drop out. He had a full complement of seven when it finally came to making the decision, but Joe insisted I come anyway. For the comfort of all, it would have been better had I been left ashore—eight bodies in a thirty-two-foot-long boat for four-and-a-half days results in very tight quarters, and there really wasn't enough sail handling for eight of us to do.

At breakfast the day of the race, Ed Botterell, a longtime friend and shipmate who runs the Hood sail loft in Canada, with a note of incredulity in his voice, asked, "Jones, do you realize that this boat is only *thirty-two feet long?* Do you mean to tell me that you are willing to sail to Bermuda in anything so small?" We laughed.

"I'm serious, gawddammit," Botterell continued, although we didn't believe him, "you and I should be on a sixty-footer, at least, let these other, less experienced mo-

The Bermuda Races

rons go to sea in a thirty-two-foot boat if they want to, but you and I have more sense."

And so it went all the way through breakfast—during which Ed was served half a grapefruit sliced the wrong way and almost impossible to eat (served him right!)—down Thames Street to Williams & Manchester, where *Robin Too* was docked, and climbing aboard—me for the first time. "Botts" kept up a running barrage on the miniscule size of our yacht. In fact, when we got there he refused to get aboard. Standing on the dock, looking down at the boat he said, "Look at that, it's too small. McBrien, I'm not coming. I'm not sailing to Bermuda on any *thirty-two-foot* boat."

I wasn't sure what Ed's motivation was except, perhaps, that he did have genuine apprehensions about the voyage upon which we were about to embark. I suppose he would have led an insurrection if he had received any support, but he kept his objections in a humorous vein and none of us took him seriously. We had some good laughs, soon Ed was aboard, and we were on our way.

By 1974 we had available before the race such sophisticated Gulf Stream detectors as infrared satellite photos, and "we" Canadians felt we possessed a slight edge in the form of this and other information provided exclusively for us by the Royal Canadian Air Force. Joe and I felt confident that we could dope out what was happening to us once we reached the Stream, both of us having continued studying how to play water temperatures to find meanders.

The information we had, indicated that there was a meander just west of the rhumb-line course. Past experience and reports from research conducted by Woods Hole and others indicated that meanders always move in an easterly direction, so our strategy was to head for a point slightly east of where the satellite photographs showed the meander to be in hopes that we would intercept the Stream at that point two days later. There had been some faint rumbling among knowledgeable navigators and skippers that the meander was supposed to move west, but we disregarded this information as being contrary to all the rules we knew of Gulf Stream behavior. We were wrong.

When we got to where we thought the Stream should be, we encountered a thoroughly confusing set of temperature readings—a very gradual rise. Joe and I conferred after a couple of hours of slowly increasing temperature readings and deduced that the Stream was west of us. Joe ordered us about and we sailed on port tack at ninety degrees to the course to Bermuda for two hours with no change in water temperature. In desperation, Joe decided to return to starboard tack. One cannot waste two hours going nowhere and still hope to place in a sailboat race, he reasoned. We had blown it in any event even if we did find the meander at this point, and if we shouldn't come to it, we would be worse off. Dejectedly, we brought *Robin Too* about and resigned ourselves to "also ran" status in the race. (For consolation we were the first boat of the Canadian Onion Patch team.)

Joe salvaged one minor triumph out of the ashes of our despair. We were both certain that we had interpreted the water temperatures correctly, that there was a meander to the west of us somewhere. In fact, that turned out to be an accurate deduction. However, the information coming as late as it did was of no value to us for the race. Loran might have helped us more, but it was our rejection of the notion that the meander could move from east to west that did us in. Had we headed for the spot we knew the meander to be in two days before—as most of the winners did—we would have been okay.

In many ways this was a typical Bermuda Race. The wind was forward of abeam on the starboard tack most of the way, the days were warm and the nights comfortable. *Robin Too* sailed along smartly, headed for her rendezvous with the Gulf Stream.

The Bermuda Races

When I went below for my first off-watch rest, I discovered that the starboard chainplate—which was just above my bunk—was leaking from water splashed on deck. The sleeping bag was wet through over about a third of its area, and the mattress underneath was soaked over the same area. Had it been rainwater, it would not have been serious, but fabric wet by seawater never completely dries, and I looked forward to the prospect of sleeping in a wet bunk for the next four days. There was nothing I could do about what was already wet, but I could try to do something to keep the bunk from getting any wetter. Stopping the leak from on deck was out of the question. We might have gotten a silacon sealent to work if the leak could have been dried out, but at sea that was impossible. Instead, I tried to divert the stream. I located some plastic sheeting which I taped to the overhead with duct tape. This made a channel over the bunk to the mast where the water should have dribbled harmlessly into the bilge. However, a couple of watches later, when *Robin* heeled more, the water from the channel found its way into the bunk shared by Jack Beetson and Tupper Hale. Rather than tear down my channel, Tupper located more plastic and more duct tape and created a channel of his own. Eventually, this water ended up on the chart table in small quantities, only Joe couldn't figure out where it was coming from, which amused the rest of us greatly—children having a laugh at the expense of the authority figure. McBrien: "Goddammit, there's water on the charts again. Where in hell is it coming from?" To which whomever was in earshot would reply, "I dunno Joe, everything in the boat is wet." Which, of course, was true.

The Gulf Stream, when we did eventually enter it, was more violent than I had ever seen it although the winds were not unusually strong. Below, trying to rest, on the afternoon of the third day, I was all too aware of *Robin*'s wild motion. It was so bad that I finally struggled out of my bunk and went on deck to find Ed Botterell straining to keep the boat under control. "A little bouncy down there, Jonesy?" Ed shouted. I replied that it was even rougher than I had imagined and got the standard routine, "... you should have been up here a few minutes ago..."

While the wind was not more than twenty-five or thirty knots, the seas were wild. They were no more than forty or forty-five feet from crest to crest, on average, and were as much as fifteen feet from crest to trough, in the extreme. *Robin*'s thirty-two-foot length barely fit between them, and it was necessary to correct her helm continually to prevent her from leaping off the tops of the waves into space.

Soon it was my watch's turn to take over, and since I had been the first on deck I relieved Botterell. I hadn't been on the helm for five minutes when a wave crest rose up without warning directly in front of us. I flashed back to *Astral,* fourteen years before. It was the same circumstance, except this time I had *not* given in to fatigue. This time there was absolutely nothing I could do, the wave just appeared in our path, and I was powerless to do anything but shout a warning and hang on.

Robin's bow thrust into the air over the peak of the crest. There was nothing on either side of the bow for many feet below, and on the other side it was a full fifteen feet to the trough below. Larry Houston was sitting on deck and reached behind to grasp the spinnaker pole. As he did so, he could see half of *Robin*'s hull leaping clear of the water, and then we fell, the bow pitching violently downward as the crest moved under our stern. The force of the crash smashed the spinnaker pole down on Larry's fingers, crushing them (fortunately not severely) between pole and deck. *Robin* shuddered, solid water on her foredeck, then she lept forward again to meet the next wave while I tried to regain my composure at the wheel and assess what had happened. Reflecting back on that moment—which is as indelibly etched in my mind's eye as

The Bermuda Races

is the almost identical incident aboard *Astral*—I could see no way that I could have avoided that wave. One second the water was almost flat in front of us, the next second a mountain rose up under us.

We continued sailing, of course, and signs of damage gradually appeared. We noticed an arclike crack in the deck a couple of feet forward of the mast. At first we didn't relate this to the crash, we couldn't understand how it had happened. Then investigation below showed that the deck had been pulled down around the mast partner, and that this probably caused the crack on deck. But how did this happen?

Robin Too was built with the diesel engine in the middle of the boat. It is directly under the mast which is supported by a stainless-steel cage built around the engine. *Robin,* like many boats, had a rod connecting the mast partner to the mast to keep the deck from lifting, and neither the rod nor its connections were altered. The only conclusion that made any sense was that we had bent the steel cage that supported the heel of the mast, and that the whole rig had moved down about an inch.

Typical of most Bermuda races, we were on starboard tack the whole way (except for our meander-hunting tack the second day). Several of us noticed that the leeward rigging appeared to be more slack than it should have been, but the mast was straight, so we did nothing about it. We discussed tying the leeward rigging off with a sailstop to keep it from moving quite so much, but the lethargy of a rough passage overpowered our good judgment. None of us did anything. We had a few anxious moments when we tacked for Kitchen Shoals near Bermuda, but everything was okay. We had survived two more days of rough weather, the rig had stood without any signs of trouble, so we shrugged and forgot about it.

A few days after our arrival, Joe asked me to go aboard *Robin* and have a look at something he had discovered with the steering. He had been preparing to sail

Robin back to Newport, and noticed that the steering cables seemed slack. Investigating, he discovered that a plate bolted to the afterside of the cockpit to hold the top rudder bearing had pulled aft at the top and had partially fractured the plywood of the cockpit side. The force of a crash must have strained the rudder mountings.

Joe dug out an aluminum plate which he had acquired for various emergency repair possibilities, and I helped him bolt it in place to reinforce the cockpit side and back up the rudder-bearing plate. When we finished we were quite proud of our work and figured it was, if anything, stronger than the original.

Most of the crew departed for home—replacements for the passage back having arrived from Canada—and secure in the belief that *Robin* was once again fit for sea, Joe and his new shipmates cast off for Newport. It was several weeks before I spoke with Joe again, and the tale of their adventures on the trip home brought into focus just how much damage we had done to *Robin* when we fell off the wave in the Gulf Stream. The following account was written up in *Yacht Racing* after several telephone interviews with McBrien. Unlike the other tales in this book, it is not a personal experience, but I was so closely involved with the events that caused the accidents, and it is such a good example of how disaster can be overcome by good preparation, that I have included it here at the end of this long chapter about the Bermuda race. It contains many lessons for everyone who sails offshore.

ON LOSING A MAST ON THE WAY HOME*

At 1115 on Tuesday, July 2, *Robin Too* was about halfway on the return between Bermuda and Newport when her helmsman reported steering difficulties. The wind

---
***Yacht Racing,* September, 1974, p. 54.

velocity was about thirty knots and the sea condition rough and quite confused, but *Robin Too* had been sailing comfortably on a reach with the number-four genoa and single-reefed mainsail.

The top bearing plate of the rudder shaft had come adrift and the rudder was threatening to tear through the hull.

Skipper McBrien ordered sails lowered and warps streamed. With the yacht lying as comfortably as possible, lines were passed around the top of the post. With the use of a handy-billy to the mast, the sideways movement of the rudder was limited and eventually brought under control. Complete repairs were made subsequently and the steering system gave no further trouble.

As potentially serious as this failure was, it was dealt with relatively routinely and was but a prelude to the greater difficulties to come.

McBrien was impressed by the incredible strength of the fiberglass hull and the ease with which it accommodated the twisting stress. While the hull cracked, there was no leaking.

By about 1415 sail was reset, and *Robin Too* was once again under way with number-four and reefed main. Although the wind had moderated somewhat, it was still rough and McBrien thought a hot meal and a bit of relaxation were in order for the crew. The wind was now from the southwest, between twenty and twenty-five knots.

About fifty minutes later—or approximately 1615—McBrien happened to be the only one below when there was a loud crack. He saw the engine box—through which the mast was stepped—waving around inside the cabin. The port upper-shroud toggle at the chainplate had failed. Instantly the port lower shroud broke at the mast, and the mast went down to horizontal—intact—ripping up the deck as it went, "just like a bloody crowbar," said McBrien. The mast then buckled halfway between the step and the deck and broke above the deck between the winches, but not before the butt had jumped out of the step and hit the underside of the deck on the port side and cracked and splintered the deck from the partners to the rail on the starboard side.

"Should we try to keep the mast?" McBrien asked himself, "and then I thought, no, in this lumpy sea somebody is going to get hurt if we start to wrestle that jagged end on board—so I elected to get rid of it." Having made this decision, big visegrips (put aboard for another purpose) were used to pull the cotter pins from the cleavis pins holding the remaining toggles to the chainplates. The end of the cleavis pins were then "wacked" with the visegrips and driven out of the toggles. This proved to be faster than sawing through the rod rigging. A hacksaw was used to cut the running rigging and the mast away.

Having a hacksaw and good blades was great," said McBrien, "but I wouldn't go again without four of them because only one guy could saw at a time (there was an incredible number of wires in the mast) and we were afraid of losing our only saw." He would also put leather thongs on the handles that could be looped around the user's wrists.

Mast, boom mainsail, Number-four genoa, all standing rigging (except part of the port lower), and halyards went over the side with the mast. Two spinnaker poles on deck were saved. McBrien considered trying to save the boom, but by the time it was thought of, it was about the only thing holding the mast to the yacht. The boom was attached at the gooseneck with bolts and by a solid vang system. To try to cut through these, near the jagged end of the mast, would have been too dangerous, in McBrien's opinion.

By 1725 the rig was cleared, and by 1930 a jury rig with the two spinnaker poles was functional. *Robin Too*'s position at 1725 was about 37°03'N 67°42'W. Almost exactly halfway between Bermuda and Newport.

McBrien had no doubt that they could make port with the jury rig and the day's worth of fuel that remained in the tanks. It would have taken quite a while, however,

The Bermuda Races

and with the prospect of wives reporting them overdue by Friday, he elected to call for help. The single sideband, high-frequency set, which had given us trouble on the race, was readjusted in Bermuda and checked as far out as thirty miles. No other station could be raised, however. The VHF set's antenna had gone over the side with the mast; although this set—with a coat-hanger antenna—was useful later, it was no help then.

With no one injured, plenty of food and water, McBrien realized that they were not in a "Mayday" situation. However, initiation of a search was probable by Friday or Saturday, and such a search mission would necessarily have to cover a wide area. With these considerations in mind, McBrien elected to use the Narco emergency beacon loaned to each yacht for the Bermuda Race by the manufacturer. The set was turned on at 1800 and appeared to function, but McBrien checked it by tuning in 121.5 Mhz (VHF emergency frequency) on a portable aircraft RDF he "happened" to have aboard. A loud and clear signal was heard blasting out on 121.5, and with that reassurance, the engine was started and *Robin Too* began making "economical cruise" progress of about 3 1/2 knots generally west to return toward the Bermuda-Newport rhumb line.

At approximately 2015 a U.S. Coast Guard aircraft was overhead, having homed in on the Narco beacon. Communications could not be established (*Robin Too*'s VHF would receive but not transmit, and the aircraft had no VHF) until a radio was dropped in a waterproof cannister, and that didn't work until it was rapped sharply against the cockpit. By midnight a rendezvous had been set up for noon next day 37°53'N 68°45'W with the CG cutter *Vigilant* (a 210-foot helicopter patrol vessel) through the aircraft communicating with its base. *Robin Too* set off under power for the rendezvous point, and the aircraft flew home. Watches were set and the crew was able to get some much-needed rest.

McBrien was able to raise the *Vigilant* on VHF radio

when it became apparent that *Robin Too* could not reach the rendezvous on time due to a four-knot adverse Gulf Stream current (the southerly meander?). They missed by about eighteen miles, but were able to steer intercepting courses.

Robin Too's crew emptied their five jerry cans of spare water (they still had fifty gallons in the main tanks), rinsed them with stove alcohol to remove the moisture, and passed them to the *Vigilant* for diesel fuel. Topping the main tank and two additional cans from the *Vigilant* gave them about fifty gallons, with McBrien calculating that they would need thirty-five to get to Newport. From the rendezvous they powered to Newport—the *Vigilant* shadowing them and communicating on VHF through the coat-hanger antenna—without further incident.

Summarizing the points that he learned from this experience, McBrien said:

"First, I'd never go to sea without at least four hacksaws—the big cutters are absolutely useless on the shrouds—all with good tungsten carbide blades and thongs so a guy can slip it over his wrist." The hacksaw worked well even on the stranded wire of the halyards.

"Second," said McBrien, "I would, for sure, have a spare VHF antenna and a length of coax cable. Stick it up on the top of a boat hook, and you have a good radio.

"The next conclusion is the question of a radar reflector—something you know is going to work, because it's stupid when you have the *Vigilant* two miles away and they can't see you on radar with your corner reflector twenty feet above the water."

It was impossible to assess the reasons for the various difficulties experienced by *Robin Too*. Ted Hood had the broken toggle part analyzed to determine the reason for its failure, and it is suspected that the crash when *Robin Too* fell off the wave on the way to Bermuda may have contributed to both rudder and rigging failures. McBrien emphasized that he thought *Robin Too* was strongly built and adequately designed for a Bermuda Race.

SOON

In 1976 I was too busy trying to put my own boat together to consider sailing to Bermuda. Besides, I was becoming increasingly impatient with the race sponsors for their refusal to allow Loran to be used. They did make a concession allowing its use early in the race and to assist making the landfall near Bermuda (some had criticized the committee, pointing out that the reefs north of Bermuda make the approach quite dangerous—use of Loran would be an added safety factor). However, the committee steadfastly refused to allow the use of Loran in the Gulf Stream. As long as they persist in this policy many will consider the Bermuda Race—as a race—an exercise in futility. Too much is left to luck. The outcome depends upon where one enters the Gulf Stream and what affect its current has on each yacht. In order to win, one must hit it right. By what logic, then, can the committee prohibit the use of a piece of equipment that is already installed in a vast majority of the racing yachts and which could provide information about the affects of the Gulf Stream's currents? I registered my frustration and protested by not going—a gesture which no one noticed, I am sure.

One day in early spring, 1978, I received a message from Humphrey Simson. "I have put you down as a watch captain for the Bermuda Race," the message said. Should I go? Why not. It would be fun to sail with Hump again. His new *Kittiwake*—which Alan Gurney designed for him in 1972—is a good boat, comfortable, not a racing machine. I would let Hump worry about the position of the Gulf Stream and enjoy the ride, wherever it took us. Unfortunately, I could not also do the Block Island Race or Newport Race Week. Both Hump and I agreed that I would have to race with the crew at least once before the Bermuda Race, and since that was apparently impossible, I canceled with genuine regret.

I shall have to do another Bermuda Race soon.

VII

Sailing Transatlantic

How many people have an opportunity to sail across the North Atlantic Ocean? But then, how many people would *want* to sail transatlantic given the opportunity. I wanted to, but I had difficulty imagining how I would go about it.

My daydreams started in 1963 with the news that the Royal Danish Yacht Club was sponsoring a race from Bermuda to Copenhagen in 1966 to commemorate the 100th anniversary of their club. I made up my mind then that I was going to go. I didn't know with whom or how I would arrange to be away from home, family, and work for most of the summer, but I was going to do it—somehow.

I had been with *Popular Boating* magazine for about a year when it was announced that our publisher had resigned and that Sydney Rogers would replace him. Syd was introduced to the staff early in June of '63, but it was explained that since he had a "previous commitment" to sail in the Transatlantic Race he wouldn't be joining the magazine until August. How nice, I thought, if Syd can take a couple of months to go sailing—especially when it meant leaving the magazine "rudderless" for two issues—he could hardly object to my doing so three years later when the race to Denmark came up. Logical though this line of thought may be, I wonder if it would have worked.

Sailing Transatlantic

I did not have to test the plan. I received an offer to join *One-Design & Offshore Yachtsman* magazine the fall of '65, and taking my inspiration from Syd I told *O-D&OY*'s publisher, Knowles Pittman, that "I had a previous commitment to sail in the Transatlantic Race...", and it was settled.

Humphrey Simson's new forty-seven-footer, designed by Gurney and built in aluminum by Robert E. Derecktor—a well-known East Coast boatbuilder—had been launched in '65 (as mentioned in the previous chapter) and the plan was to race in the Southern Ocean Racing Circuit (SORC) in the winter of '66 as a warm-up for the Bermuda and Transatlantic Races that summer.

We did well in the Circuit, finishing a close series tied for third place with Pat Haggerty's *Bay Bea* and beaten by S. K. Wellman's *Indigo* (second) and Ted Turner's Cal-40 *Vamp X* (first). All would be class rivals in the Transatlantic Race. *Kittiwake* proved up to the challenge in every way, but a couple of potential crew members did not.

The first rejected applicant sailed with us in the first two SORC races. He was a pleasant fellow and quite capable. We didn't know until soon after the start of the Saint Petersburg to Fort Lauderdale Race when we sailed into the rough water of the Gulf of Mexico that he had a physical disability. On the foredeck to change headsails, our potential transatlantic crew member dislocated his shoulder. This had happened to him before, and fortunately he knew what to do to put it back. However, it took several tries by a couple of us to restore the joint to its socket. Finally, at his instruction, with my foot in his armpit, I pulled on his wrist with all my strength. When he grunted "twist," I did, and the arm went back with a thump where it belonged—the "operation" being performed in wet oilskins in a dark, bouncing cabin. Of course, he was available for only limited duty for the rest of the race. Although he assured us that he could restrict the movement of his arm to prevent a recurrence, we thought we'd prefer not to sail transatlantic with someone who had a built-in disability—our lives and his might depend upon all of us being able to use both arms. It was a tough choice, because he was otherwise a good shipmate.

Another reject rejected himself after we got to Bermuda. I had been wooing Alan MacDonald, who runs a very successful yacht-rigging service in Stamford, Connecticut, to race with us. Alan was interested, but he decided that he could not take the time. Coincidentally we replaced Alan *Mac*Donald with Alan *Mc*Donald, who had been recommended by a mutual friend. We got along fine with the "new" Alan, and he learned *Kittiwake*'s "ropes" quickly. Alan sailed on the other watch to Bermuda, and I was totally unaware of how unhappy he was. Granted, it was a difficult race with none of us getting much rest, and, to his credit, Alan pulled his share. Only when we were safely in Hamilton harbor did he confess to Humphrey that ocean sailing was not for him. Reluctantly, he had reached the decision not to continue on to Copenhagen. We found a willing and experienced replacement, whom we thought for a while was another Mac/McDonald, in Dave *Mc*Farlane.

Organizing for a Transatlantic Race is more complicated than a Bermuda Race by an order of magnitude of ten or more. Considering that one has an extremely limited amount of space and that everything that eight people will need to survive for a minimum of three weeks must be provided on board, the planning and organization must be near flawless—life depends upon it. Each meal must be planned, supplies bought and stowed. What happens if through some misfortune it takes an additional three weeks to reach land? *Emergency* stores must be planned, bought, and stowed. How long will eggs keep? Milk? Bread? How do you cope with a hole in the hull—unlikely in an aluminum hull three-sixteenths of an inch

Sailing Transatlantic

thick, but you think about it. Man overboard? You think about the father and two sons who were lost in the Transatlantic Race in 1935.* Suppose someone breaks a bone or has an appendicitis attack. What about fuel for the stove, heat for the cabin—where we were going the average water temperature in July is fifty-six degrees Fharenheit. Sails: how do you mend them? How do you cope with chafe?

Each of these considerations and many more had to be thought about, planned for, and accommodated in some way. For example, we had a special antitripping reef put into the mainsail. Hardly required now with the trend toward short booms, this rig consisted of a special set of reef points and leach cringle, angling up from the tack of the sail. When tied in, this reef raised the outboard end of the boom to prevent it from digging into the water on a downwind roll to leeward. In addition, we made and rigged a special "preventer"; a wire leading from the end of the boom to the bow. If the boom should go in the water with a vang set and no preventer, the vang would resist the aft movement of the boom and most likely bend the boom or break the gooseneck. These two precautions avoided all difficulty. In fact, in the entire transatlantic passage we didn't have a single gear failure (not counting my error in judgment allowing us to carry the light spinnaker in too much wind—it split from luff to leech!).

In addition to the important things to plan for, there are more mundane items to consider when planning a 3,600-mile passage. What, for instance, do you do about laundry? Do you wash soiled underwear or do you try to stow it somewhere? Our solution was taken from Fred Adams's *Katama* (with whom Syd Rogers had sailed in '63); each of us brought a supply of cheap shorts, T-shirts, and socks, and after wearing them for two days we simply

---

*Alfred F. Loomis, *Ocean Racing* rev. ed. (New York: Yachting Publishing Corp., 1946), p. 213.

heaved them over the side. Imagine eight people's accumulation of dirty underwear after twenty-one days at sea!

One very important consideration was what to do about food and preparing it. In short races we had found it unnecessary to have a full-time cook on a boat *Kittiwake*'s size. Even going to Bermuda we found that by preparing roasts and casseroles ashore and then freezing them, we could eat varied and relatively fancy meals without anyone having to slave over a hot stove all day. On a Long Island Sound race Humphrey once served the crew brazed guinea hen he had shot, cooked, and frozen the previous fall—now that's elegant. However, for a race which will take three weeks, we had to make other arrangements.

How well a crew eats has a magnified affect on morale. After two weeks of canned spagetti, shipmates might tend to develop short tempers—little incidents being exaggerated out of proportion. Conversely, a well-fed crew which has been served a variety of meals—something to look forward to each day—can be expected to remain relatively serene, other things being equal.

Considering these things, which we had learned from others who had made similar trips—the *Figaro* incident told to Barney and me (Chapter VI) was well remembered in spite of our inebriated state when we heard it—we decided to seek an experienced offshore cook to add to our crew.

Alan Gurney, who sailed with us in the SORC but was sailing with George Moffett transatlantic, had received a letter from Joan McKee, a longtime English friend and outstanding sea cook. Joan wrote Alan about someone I'll call "Dilly" who was also from England, very experienced, and wanted a berth for the Bermuda and Transatlantic Races. Alan surmised that if Joan was recommending this person she must be good, and it was settled when Alan and I had breakfast in Nassau with

Skip Shaw, who had sailed with Dilly previously.* Skip said she was an excellent cook and a good shipmate. He recommended her without reservation. That settled it. Humphrey wrote to Dilly in England and offered her the job.

Dilly arrived in May in time to help organize *Kittiwake*. She stayed with the Simsons at their home in Connecticut—many miles from the water—and after a short time became outspokenly impatient with this arrangement. On her previous visit to the U.S. she had stayed aboard a boat at the Seawanhaka Corinthian Yacht Club in Oyster Bay, Long Island, had been surrounded by fellow sailors, and swamped by the social whirl. *Kittiwake* spent an overly long time in Derecktor's boatyard being refitted following the SORC, and there wasn't much for Dilly to do. She couldn't understand that Humphrey and the rest of us had jobs—plus trying to organize being away for six weeks—and couldn't spend two or three weeks lazing about in Oyster Bay.

When we finally got *Kittiwake* sailing again it was with great relief. Here, at last, was something for Dilly to do. Unfortunately, she proved not to live up to her advance billing—at least as far as her sailing ability was concerned. She couldn't steer a straight line at the wheel, and she didn't know the mainsheet from the spinnaker halyard. We hoped she could cook better than she could sail, and decided to try her out on the Bermuda Race. Then, if she didn't work out, Humphrey would give her her plane ticket back to England and we'd either do without a cook or try to line one up in Bermuda.

Dilly was pretty good going to Bermuda. She was much more cheerful, she cooked willingly, and her meals

---

*We conferred with Joan after the race, and Joan confessed she had not known Dilly well. Alan agreed, in hindsight, that Joan's letter had not been a "recommendation." She only reported that Dilly was available. Our imagination and desire for another "Joan McKee" colored our judgment.

were satisfactory. We decided that all she needed was to get to sea. She'd work out fine on the Transatlantic.

Once ashore at Bermuda, Dilly reverted to her previous ways and added a couple more aberrations to our list. At a social function ashore she stripped off her dress in the middle of a cocktail party and dove into the host's pool. She *was* wearing a bikini underneath her dress (she had two—one pink and one baby blue—which, as far as we knew, were all she ever wore for underwear), but such conduct was not up to the social standards of the Bermudians.

Supplies presented many logistic problems from Bermuda. Dry ice, which is used to extend the life of regular ice for things which have to be kept cool (like meat, butter, and some fresh vegetables) had to be especially flown in from the U.S. Other things, such as canned bread, also had to be imported, and careful planning was needed in obtaining local supplies.

Humphrey's wife, Posie, helped considerably in planning *Kittiwake*'s victuals. One day Humphrey discovered that Dilly had sent back several boxes of food Posie had ordered from the grocer in Hamilton. We had agreed in advance what we wanted to eat, and these things we had all agreed we liked in common. Dilly sent them back—saying they weren't needed. Steve Lang, who liked almost nothing but peanut butter, would not have survived the trip if Dilly had succeeded in returning the dozen jars Posie had obtained.

Even with these differences we decided to stick with Dilly. After all, she had worked out fine on the Bermuda Race, and once we were back at sea everything would be okay. What we didn't discover until later—after it was too late—was that on the Bermuda Race Dilly had secreted a bottle of gin in the galley, and this apparently helped maintain her high spirits. With every inch of space used and accounted for on the Transatlantic Race, and with what grog we had (Teddy Gosling's Old Barbados rum)

Skipper Humphrey Simson scratches his head in wonder at the mountain of stores which must be put aboard *Kittiwake* before the start of the Transatlantic Race.

under the control of the skipper, Dilly had no opportunity to hide a private stash. For better or worse, she was to be our cook for the next three weeks.

The period between the finish of the Bermuda Race and the start of the Transatlantic Race was very pleasant for me. Humphrey and Posie stayed ashore with friends, and Barney Compton and I found an apartment ashore which we rented at a very favorable rate. This gave us freedom from *Kittiwake* and, I'm sure, made it more pleasant for those who were staying aboard. There wasn't much to do except to arrange for the straightening of a bent spinnaker pole and have an automobile body repairman replace a patch of fairing compound that had fallen from *Kittiwake*'s starboard bow. There were few repairs necessary of the type we could do ourselves, so we were free to explore the island, enjoy the beaches, and make friends among the natives and fellow tourists. It was a period of serenity that was very beneficial psychologically. By starting time I was psyched and ready to undertake an adventure which, before the fact, was awesome in scope—to sail for nineteen to twenty-one days thirty-six hundred miles across a trackless ocean to a legendary land I had never seen!

We started in a gale. It was raining and blowing up to forty knots from the east-northeast—on the nose. What a way to start a Transatlantic Race! Normally, I would have found the prospect of being wet and uncomfortable in the stormy, bouncing sea a bit depressing—especially at the beginning of such a long voyage. I have never been seasick in the normal sense, but it has always taken a couple of days for me to overcome the lethargy brought on by the unusual motion. Now I was fearless. Bring on the storm, we are sailing transatlantic into the unknown ocean. Let me at it!

Humphrey had asked me to be starting helmsman, and in my eagerness to begin the race I put *Kittiwake* over the line early. My unfortunate shipmates had to cope with an extra jibe and tack in the raging storm, and we started our thirty-six-hundred-mile race a mile behind our class rivals.

When sailing to windward, the drain in *Kittiwake*'s head basin had a tendency to back up into the basin. Water forced up the pipe would lift the stopper, which if in the closed position would prevent the water from running down the drain again. It was a sort of reverse pump action. We knew about this, of course, and normally sailed with the seacock shut. However, after many days in port, we had forgotten to close the seacock. Coincidentally, we had stowed our entire supply of eggs in the otherwise unused laundry hamper located under the counter outboard of the basin. I happened to be the first one to go into the head a few hours after the start, and what I found was a hamper full of a gooey mixture of seawater, the pulp of egg cartons, broken egg shells, and egg yokes and whites. Such a discovery would normally have sent me hurrying on deck, if not to bolt for the rail then close to it. However, in my euphoria to be under way I found I could be stoical about my discovery and set about cleaning it up. It took the better part of an hour with pans and buckets, pumping the mess through the head—*Kittiwake* thrashing and bouncing to windward—and when I was finished all that could be salvaged from fourteen dozen eggs was an even dozen. So much for eggs for breakfast; we would have to do without.

As mentioned in a previous chapter, *Kittiwake* was an outstanding performer on the wind in heavy going. I never understood what combination of characteristics made her so good in the conditions we were experiencing the first two days of the Transatlantic Race, but we were soon well in the lead of our class, our starting deficit completely erased. By the time the gale blew itself out and the weather settled down to normal, we had a sixty-mile lead in Class C.

We saw only two competitors during the first week of

the race and none thereafter until the finish. Both were in Class B; *Jan Pott* was a fifty-foot German yawl and the French schooner, *Pen Duick II. Pen Duick* was sailing a course very different from ours, which puzzled us at the time. We learned later that she had suffered rudder damage and was retiring to the French island of Saint Pierre off the coast of Newfoundland. There were three other early retirements—our rival *Indigo* had lost her centerboard during the storm the second day, and the other American yachts *Dutch Treat* and *Burgoo* quit for unspecified reasons.

We saw one other vessel, one of two small boats which were attempting to row across the Atlantic. We spoke briefly with the boat crewed by David Johnstone and John Hoare. They appeared to be in good spirits and told us all was well. They were never seen again.* The other boat with Chay Blyth and John Ridgway aboard, which we did not see, subsequently completed their passage to England successfully.†

Some of the competitors had arranged to report their daily positions by radio to Henry B. duPont's *Cyane,* which provided radio contact with the rest of the world. This position reporting was not obligatory, and we had originally decided not to participate. However, we tuned in and listened for a couple of days—which is how we found out we were sixty miles in the lead—and decided to join in. While we derisively referred to these daily transmissions as "children's hour," it was interesting to plot everyone's progress and to hear how other yachts were fairing.

Our great circle course (an arc if traced on a globe but appearing as a curved line when plotted on a flat chart) took us almost due north from Bermuda to within about

---

*John Ridgway and Chay Blyth, *A Fighting Chance* (Philadelphia and New York: J. B. Lippincott Company, 1967), p. 211.
†Ibid.

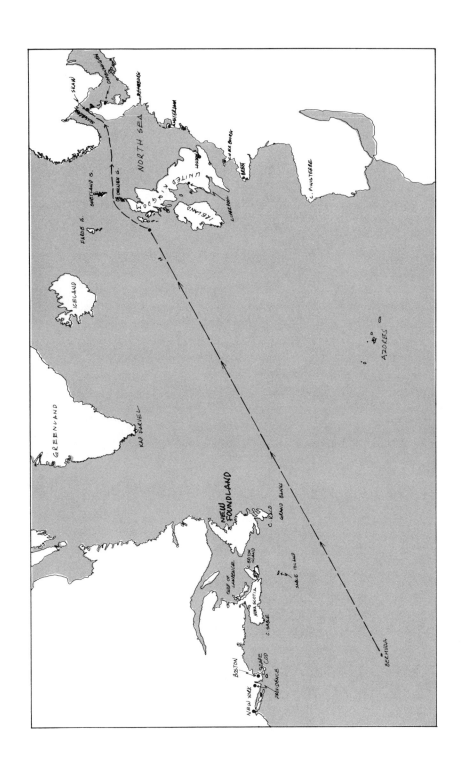

a hundred miles of Newfoundland. From there it is about twenty-five hundred miles to Rockall, a pinnacle of rock off Great Britain which lay directly on our course, thence to the north of the Orkney Islands above Scotland, across the North Sea past the tip of Norway to the finish at Skagen (Skaw) lightship.

When the gale blew itself out, it left behind the expected southwesterly winds of twenty-five to thirty-five knots which saw us surfing along under spinnaker for day after day. This was glorious sailing before the wind under either the full-size 1.5-ounce spinnaker or the smaller 2.2-ounce storm spinnaker. Day and night, watch and watch we flew. The further north and east we went, the harder it blew and the colder it got. Soon the days were noticeably longer. Under such idyllic conditions time, except for reckoning the half-hourly wheel tricks and the four-, five-, or six-hour watches, became meaningless. What day is it; Sunday? Monday? Wednesday? Who knows? Who cares!

Kittiwake, being one of the last of the breed of ocean racers with the rudder attached to the keel, was difficult to keep under control downwind under these conditions. Every few minutes the helmsman would lose control momentarily, and she'd round up to windward or off to leeward dumping her spinnaker. We got quite used to this action which would have been so rare in sheltered waters as to cause panic. It became a contest among helmsman to see if they could steer a whole half-hour wheel watch without losing it. We decided that those who were successful should belong to the "No Flop Club." To acknowledge membership in this exclusive group, I made labels with a Dymo labelmaker which those of us who had earned them wore proudly on our foul-weather jackets or caps. Those who were able to perform the feat a second time were issued a "+" and soon we all had "No Flop Club" badges with many plus-signs beneath. When we got so good that this game became meaningless, we started the "10+ Club" for those who had pushed *Kittiwake* past the ten-knot limit on her speedometer. At first, it was almost impossible to get a confirmed 10+, but as the wind and seas built up, we were all soon members with many plus-sign clusters.

We felt really confident that we could stay ahead of all in our class but Ted Turner's Cal-40. We knew that she would be flying in these conditions (in fact, for every 10 + that we'd register she was registering twelve to fourteen), but we were relying on some stormy weather in the notorious North Sea to allow us to catch her. Alas, it was not to be. Still, we were reasonably confident as we maintained our sixty-mile lead every day during "children's hour."

Humphrey had one frustrating day during which it appeared we had lost our lead. The day before, Barney woke up our watch in great frustration. "Something's terribly wrong, Teddy," he was saying to me even before I was on deck. "We're really going slowly. I don't know if there's something on the keel or what. We've tried everything we can think of, and we can't get more than four knots out of her."

I was as puzzled as Barney, but I couldn't imagine we were only going four knots. When Steve Lang came on deck he looked around for a minute then disappeared below. A minute later the speedometer needle whipped around to 7 1/2. We had been sailing for so long that we had worn out the batteries which powered the Brooks & Gatehouse instruments. Steve knew what to do because he had serviced this gear when working for Patrick Ellam, the U.S. agent.

But we had forgotten this incident when Humphrey took his noon latitude. Working from the DR as calculated from the log which runs from the speedometer circuitry, Hump had made a quite logical 60-mile error. We imagined the next day when we reported our corrected position that our apparent 260-mile day's run would raise some eyebrows among the competition, but no one ever commented.

After a while I began to regret that we were in a race. Day after day of sailing without touching a sheet, except to move the chafe points, and without another competitor in sight, one begins to wonder what is the point of racing. It all seems unreal. You begin to wish you were the only boat out there and were free to fly wherever the whim of the wind would take you. I read two books while on watch during the race, and felt a nagging guilt that I should be doing this while racing. However, to deny ourselves this opportunity would have been silly. It wasn't that we were bored, there was always something to see, to enjoy, but one could still appreciate the endless surge of the sea, the incessant drive of the wind, the glory of sun, sky, and clouds while also becoming engrossed in a novel. I vowed someday to sail transatlantic again, but not in a race. There would be a purity of cruising transatlantic that might well be the ultimate sailing joy.

Dilly's cooking was quite satisfactory even in the rough conditions we experienced the first two days, but English fare was not what most of us were used to. We soon began to long for something other than artichoke hearts and hearts of palm. Each of our meals, including breakfasts, seemed to contain large quantities of onions. Coming from the "Onion Patch," as Bermuda is sometimes called, they were a natural. Onions are also good shipboard fare as they keep the digestive system in excellent trim—particularly the latter stages of it. But after almost a week of onions three times a day, I found my lower digestive tract unnecessarily active. I canvassed others of my shipmates and learned that they were experiencing similar problems. I suggested to Dilly, as tactfully as I could, that she might cut down on the onions and include them in only one meal a day (actually, I would have preferred not to see another onion for at least a week). I explained that it wasn't that I didn't like them,

Sailing Transatlantic

it was just that my system was not used to them in such quantity, and I was afraid I might blow holes in my trousers if the present rate of consumption continued.

"You don't like my cooking," Dilly wailed and flew into a rage. No amount of cajoling would turn her off, and thereafter I was on Dilly's hate list.

One by one the rest of the crew was caught by Dilly in some transgression or another—real or imagined—and she ended up not speaking civilly to any of us. Steve was the first to join me on her list. He had found that she was striking matches on the plexiglass window above the galley. Plexiglass makes an excellent striker for wooden kitchen matches, but they leave behind a deep, ugly scratch. Steve tried to explain this to Dilly in a tactful manner pointing out that plexiglass was expensive, that it was built into the boat, that a replacement was not available at sea, and that if she continued we soon wouldn't be able to see out of the window. For an answer he was thereafter treated with the cold-shoulder routine.

Steve did nothing to further ingratiate himself with our cook when he cleaned up her galley one afternoon while she was asleep. Dilly's galley continually had the appearance that a full-course meal was in the process of being prepared—even when she was in her bunk. It wasn't that dirty dishes were left around. There was simply a general clutter of this and that. One of the things Steve disposed of was a cache of "Baggy" ties. There were at least two dozen used ones sitting in an ash tray in a corner of the galley counter, and he heaved them over the side.

"Steve, you've thrown away my 'Baggy' ties," Dilly admonished in her most anguished English tones. When Steve pointed out that each new box of "Baggies" comes with a fresh supply of ties she retored with, "I was saving them for Posie." Steve simply shrugged incredulously.

Steve also tried to correct a bad habit Dilly had of shutting off the gas stove by simply turning off the master valve—the burner valves remained open. She said she would, but many times we caught her doing it improperly. We suspected that this error was the cause of later difficulty.

"Baggy" ties weren't the only things our cook collected. She started with Mike Wick, the youngest and most easily persuaded, and gradually worked through the rest of the crew. "Don't throw your underwear overboard," she told Mike, "I'll wash it for you so it won't be wasted." Of course, she never washed any of the stuff she collected. Instead, it sat in a garbage bag in a wet heap on the sole in the forward sailbin. The bag got bigger and bigger as she added dirty underwear, but never cleaner. One day I asked her to do something about it before little green things came out of the mold to take over the ship. My humor was unappreciated and ineffectual. The bag remained.

When we were two weeks out of Bermuda and just beginning to get into really cold weather, the gas for the galley stove ran out. This was a puzzle, at first, and a nasty surprise. It meant we would have no more hot food for the remainder of the race. We had a similar problem after arriving in Bermuda—one of the two tanks appeared empty, but since one tank had lasted all winter we were sure the remaining tank would see us through to Copenhagen. Trying to refill in Bermuda had been impossible anyway, so we went with the one bottle of gas and forgot about it.

We were convinced that Dilly's habit of shutting the stove off with the master valve—which we sometimes found not completely shut—had caused an intermittent leak. If we were right it was a wonder we didn't blow ourselves out of the water.

Since we were moving into an area of cold water, we decided that we could fire up the cabin charcoal heater. Hugh Calder, on Barney's watch, devised a bracket out of wire coat-hangers which we could hang inside the stove.

Hugh surmised that we could heat small cans with this rig and have at least one hot meal a day. We decided to try a can of spaghetti.

"Now Dilly," Hugh admonished, "don't forget to punch a hole in the top of the can to let the steam out."

"What do you think I am, *stupid,*" was Dilly's insulted rejoinder.

Later that afternoon, just before the change of the watch, Steve was stepping out of the pilot berth to get dressed. Boom! The cabin filled with smoke, ashes, and hot coals. The lid from the stove sailed across the cabin—hitting Steve in the back and falling into my lap on the bunk below. We scrambled around putting out the glowing coals, and when the smoke and dust had settled we could see bits of spaghetti and tomato sauce all over the cabin. Steve had reached the end of his tolerance. *"You stupid bitch,"* he shouted at Dilly. "Didn't we tell you to put a hole in the can? You could have killed us all!" "But I did put a hole in the can, I did," Dilly sobbed. Thereafter one of us supervised whenever anything was put inside the cabin heater, and we had no further trouble.

Day after day the miles were ticked off on the master North Atlantic chart to which Humphrey would transfer the daily noon positions from his plotting sheets, and as the wind hauled around toward the west we were forced to jibe. There is an old Transatlantic Race "saw" that goes, "When shall we jibe, on Wednesday or Thursday, decisions, decisions!" This was, literally, our choice. We put it off as long as possible.

Soon, as we reached the lattitude of Scotland, the nights were only three hours long—it would be light until 2300 and the sun would show itself again at 0200. One night the wind fell away almost to nothing drawing abeam—that's when I failed to appreciate the weight of the wind, which compared to the weeks we had spent rolling before thirty-knot winds seemed light, and blew out *Kittiwake*'s light chute. Soon we were looking for

"Happy Hour," a gathering time for both watches, in mid-ocean. Captain Simson "tests" the Mount Gay and pronounces it fit for consumption while Dave McFarlane looks on from the helm—racing-edge concentration broken—and Barney Compton waits patiently.

Rockall—hoping we didn't run upon it in the night. Then we made our landfall at Saint Kilda Island—a sentinel of the Outer Hebrides. From that time on our fortunes took a downward turn.

We approached Saint Kilda in a dying wind—the closer we got the less it blew—and finally we stopped completely with the sails slatting so badly on the oily swell that we had to take them down. We made good use of the respite going forward to smooth the aluminum spinnaker pole and fitting where the wire guy had chafed a deep groove and checking out other minor points of wear and chafe.

In the morning Mike spotted something moving high atop Saint Kilda's mountain ridge. He couldn't make out any details, but we could all see, once he had pointed it out to us, that something was definitely moving way up there a thousand feet above the sea. Humphrey's charts made no mention of any kind of structure, and we began to imagine it was a windmill from an ancient monastery—the "Order of Saint Kilda"—revolving in the wind. What wind. If there were monks up there with wind why didn't they send it down to us.

Speculation continued all day as we sat almost motionless in Saint Kilda's lee. Finally we could see through the binoculars that the rotating object was a radar antenna. We had no way of knowing then the significance the radar was playing in our presence, but later Humphrey heard that a British rocket test had to be postponed for twenty-four hours because a yacht lay becalmed in the drop zone.

Everyone in our class was affected by the calm, but none suffered as much as we. The next day's "children's hour" revealed that *Bay Bea* had whittled away most of our sixty-mile lead. We were now in a desperate struggle to stay ahead of her and save our time. *Guinevere* in Class B suffered even more, posting only forty-eight miles from noon to noon.

Mike Wick makes an entry in the deck log following his trick at the helm. His next task will be to pick up where he left in the novel tucked under the log—the tough life of a Transatlantic Race crew!

The wind returned from the north, and we had a lovely close reach past the northern Hebrides and close aboard the Orkney Islands at the northern tip of Scotland. The sight of those rocky islands with their sparse vegetation, bright green grasses shining in the northern sunlight, was absolutely breathtaking. I sat transfixed in the leeward scuppers as *Kittiwake* slipped noiselessly along, close reaching on the port tack. I thought it was the most beautiful sight I had ever seen—so lonely and desolate, yet so lovely.

Under spinnaker again we ghosted into the North Sea which then went flat as a millpond. Here was to be our chance to catch Ted Turner in a couple of days hard thrash to windward. Ha! Again we lay becalmed, the kittiwake gulls swimming beside, mocking their namesake, appearing double as their images reflected in the glassy sea.

Our last few days were fitful. The coast of Norway appeared briefly in the haze to windward, and then *Solution* (Tor Ramsing's fifty-foot Class-B sloop) appeared just ahead, and could that be *Guinevere* on the horizon? Then the Skaw lightship came into view, and suddenly it was over. We had been sailing for a bit over twenty-one days and had covered over thirty-six hundred nautical miles.

The wind died as we finished, but not before *Bay Bea* finished well within her handicap on us. Turner had finished *days* before to take our class easily. We were third. *Guinevere*, despite her forty-eight-mile day was second in Class B which we envied. *Kittiwake* rated top boat in Class C, and had the committee put us as the bottom boat in Class B instead, we would have beaten *Guinevere* for second in that class. If you don't win there are always "what if's" but excuses don't count.

From the finish to Copenhagen was another full day's run, and with no wind we turned on the "diesel breeze" to motor south. Barney and I celebrated by bathing from the unused jerry cans of fresh water. It was wonderful, scampering naked and clean under the Scandanavian sun. At suppertime we celebrated with champagne and several bottles of Teddy Gosling's best. Fortunately, Steve is a nondrinker, and he stayed up the whole night steering and navigating *Kittiwake* down the Kattegat toward Helsignør. It was just as well we had no wind and no emergencies to cope with because the rest of us were in no condition to do anything. With seven of us below I found all the bunks filled and passed out on the sails in the forepeak, disgraceful!

In the morning we motored past Helsignør Castle, and I imagined I could see the ghost of Hamlet looking out from the parapets. The red-tiled roofs of Sweden glided by to port while to starboard lay the rolling pastoral fields of Denmark. I was in a Scandanavian fairytale land I'd only dreamed of before through the classic writings of William Shakespeare and Hans Christian Anderson and the classical music of Edvard Grieg and Jean Sebelius.

We arrived at Lynetten, a navy basin set aside as a harbor for visiting yachts, and there were hundreds of yachts from all over the world. Beautiful ocean racers crammed gunwale to gunwale flying the flags of Norway, Sweden, Finland, Germany, France, Holland, Belgium, England, Italy, Spain, Great Britain, the U.S., Denmark—of course—and even Australia. Soon we were caught up in it all. Humphrey, Barney, Steve, and I had rooms at a hotel, and we were happy to be away from *Kittiwake* and sailing for a while. Most of the yachts went off a few days later to sail the Skaw Race, the roughest in history in which eighty percent of the fleet was forced to withdraw. We had had enough sailing and did not regret missing this one in the least. Copenhagen beckoned—dinner with the King and Queen in Helsignør—Tivoli Gardens—shopping—the Tall Ships in review—Tuborg *Grøn* Ol—Danish sandwiches—Paul Elvstrom—trolley cars—aquavit

Day upon day of running before 30-knot winds characterized this particular Transatlantic Race. *Kittiwake* clicked off a series of 200-mile days for over a week.

and beer—Nyhavn—the little mermaid—Freddie the bartender....

One morning Humphrey and Barney decided it was time to have a look at *Kittiwake* across the harbor at Lynetten. Hugh and Dilly had been staying aboard, and Humphrey discovered to his displeasure that Dilly had invited some of her friends to stay there also. Dilly wasn't aboard. The cabin was a mess. Hugh threw up his hands in a gesture of futility then set to with Hump and Barney to clean up the cabin. They stowed unidentified belongings in one pile and threw out the rest, including the bag of dirty underwear Dilly had obtained from the crew during the race. It was still forward on the sole. Barney heaved it into the middle of a large dumpster with great satisfaction.

The next morning Dilly called Humphrey at the hotel. Angrily, she accused him of throwing away friends' belongings and especially her bag of dirty laundry. Humphrey confessed. "Well," she said triumphantly, "I climbed into the garbage and got it!"

Dilly hitched a ride home on a small English yacht, and we were told that the plastic bag of dirty underwear went with her. We pitied this crew while we wondered what in the world she was going to do with thirty or so pairs of dirty men's shorts and T-shirts.

Dilly had been an adventure for all of us. She surely hated each of us before the race was over, and with some justification. However, we all felt she brought most of it upon herself and that we had, for a while at least, tried to meet her halfway. There was one positive benefit her presence aboard had. She was the focus for any animosity the rest of us may have harbored. We took it all out on her, and never did the rest of the crew have a harsh word for anyone else.

One gets accustomed to the Atlantic rollers that surge up from astern and the wind that sends *Kittiwake* hurtling down their faces at better than 10-knots, the top of the speedometer's dial.

VIII

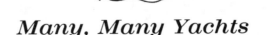

Many, Many Yachts

LIKE A FLIGHT OF GIGANTIC Snowbirds, the little boats that used to pass like a single cloud across Newport Bay, five hundred eighty offshore racers drifted past the three committee boats stationed along the mile-long starting line. In numbers of participants, the race to Ensenada, Mexico, from Newport Beach, California, is unquestionably the world's largest ocean race. Everything from Cal-24s to one hundred-foot-plus schooners may participate. It doesn't matter if they have one, two, or three hulls (no one has shown up yet with a quadrimaran). Everybody races to Ensenada, and everybody seemed to be there—including a couple of Connecticut Yankees.

Before I left home for a week in sunny California we had speculated on just how they *would* handle five hundred eighty boats on one starting line. A single class on a line from Balboa to Catalina Island was one impractical suggestion. Another speculation was dividing the fleet into ten classes, which still left the unwieldy number of sixty boats per class. Until the night before the race, I didn't dream they would start the little boats first, but I worked myself into a sleepless night thinking about the prospect of five hundred eighty boats meeting at once, on the same piece of ocean, umpteen miles down the California coast.

They do things differently in the Ensenada Race and,

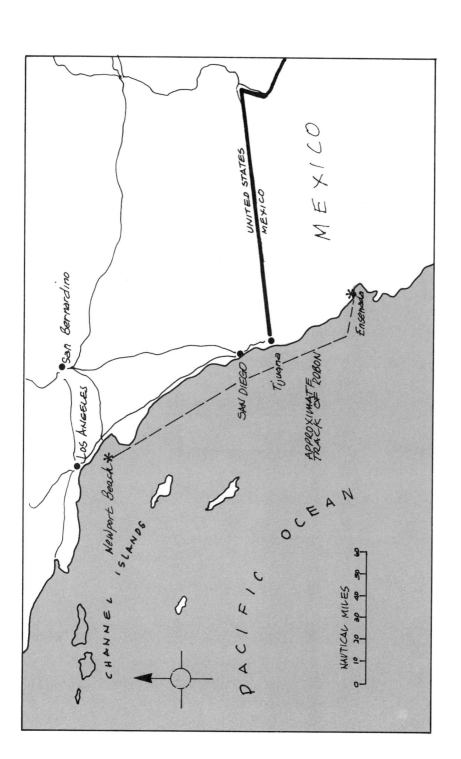

when I reported aboard Bob Grant's Columbia 50 *Robon III* the next morning, my worst fears were confirmed. Rating near the bottom of Class A, we were to start last, after Classes E,D,C, and B in two divisions—Ocean Racing and Pacific Handicap—Midget Ocean Racing Fleet and Ocean Racing Catamaran. Pacific Handicap crossed the eastern half of the line while the Ocean Racing Division used the western half. It all worked out somehow, and once I got used to the idea of forty or fifty miles of bad air it was not so bad. We had no incidents, nor did I hear of any in this race. The only "horror story" was related by Ed Warmington of the time he looked up from the tiller of his Lapworth 36 to converse with the bowsprit man—dangling fifteen feet above Ed's cockpit—from an eighty-eight-foot ketch which was overtaking him. Ed held his course as the rules required (one is not permitted to luff another boat to prevent her going past) while trying to convince the bowsprit man to pass the word aft that there was somebody in the way. Finally, with the ketch's bowsprit overlapping his backstay Ed's son poised by the rail and announced, "I'm leavin', Dad!" at which point Ed put the helm down and just barely escaped with the L-36's rig intact.

Incidentally, the no-luffing rule is a must. Imagine a Cal-25 luffing a Columbia 29 luffing an Ohlson 36 luffing a 6-Meter—all the way up to the 12-Meter *Newsboy* luffing the eighty-eight-foot scratch yawl *Saluda*. They could stretch from the Coronados to Hawaii or all jam into Mission Bay before the word passed down the line for sea room.

The Ensenada Race is different all right; with five hundred eighty boats of such varied types, it has to be unique. Amazingly, it all comes off very well. Never have I been aboard a boat that beat as many competitors in one race—or in a season!

The start was in very light headwinds which by the time Class A got under way at 12:30 PM was a close fetch

Many, Many Yachts

in a three- or four-knot southerly.

Bob Grant placed *Robon III* in position for a good if not spectacular start, and we were off for Ensenada, one hundred twenty-five miles down the coast. The spectacular start in Class A was reserved for Don Haskell's sixty-six-foot Sparkman & Stephens sloop *Chubasco. Chubby* steamed away from the line under power with ten minutes to go, then turned at the predetermined time and headed for the windward end of the line at full chat. The engine was secured at the five-minute signal, and at the gun *Chubby* nipped under the committee boat ahead of the whole class and with two-knots more way than anyone else. A really gutsy start—perfectly timed.

We were fortunate to have the wind come up and haul to the south just before our start. This put the bulk of the fleet to leeward of us and we had a minimum of interference from small fry. After we broke through *Newsboy*'s lee (the Columbia 50 wasn't really outfooting the 12-Meter, it only seemed that she was) we settled down on a rhumb-line course zigzagging only occasionally to avoid wind shadows.

After about an hour, both the breeze and the competition began to sort out, giving us a clearer picture of our position. The wind settled in to a pleasant, if not enthusiastic, five- to seven-knot southerly. The sun came out, and life was rosy. John Noble's *Simoon,* the yawl-rigged Columbia 50 and one of our close rivals, was half-a-mile astern. We seemed to be moving very well. No one near us was going faster except for several of the larger boats, *Newsboy* and *Chubasco* among them, that were standing further out to sea. Our course was plotted to take us to the Coronados Islands which lie close to the rhumb line near the California-Mexico border.

It was gratifying but relatively meaningless to sail past a succession of Cal-25s, Cal-28s, Islander and Columbia 29s and numerous other small fry. There seemed to be no end to the Cal-25s. Just when we'd think we had passed "surely the last of those" another would appear on the bow, clipping along only a half-knot or so slower than *Robon.*

Our first significant triumph came when we passed Houston Snidow's 10-Meter *Braila.* She had been sitting ahead and slightly to windward occasionally giving us a dose of bad air. Finally, *Braila* sailed further to windward, fell into a temporary hole and we slipped through her lee.

We came alongside Bob Jones's catamaran *Allez Cat* briefly as she did not like the light going. Pleasantries (sounding like the opposite) were exchanged as we had a family rivalry going—*Robon III* crew member Norm Reynolds making snide remarks to his father aboard *Allez Cat.*

Then there was the incident which I hestitate to include in a race story, but which was unique in my racing experience. Bob Grant's son Gerry had brought two pigeons aboard. They remained very quietly in a box until about 1500 when Gerry produced them on deck. With a message attached to one (the other pigeon presumably was for moral support), both were flung skyward over the sea. After a couple of orientation circles while casting wary eyes toward the curious seagulls, both pigeons disappeared, heading home to mom. The message? "I don't like baloney sandwiches. Love, Gerry."

Besides Gerry Grant, we had for crew his two brothers, Taylor and Larry, and Norm Reynolds. These four comprised our muscle power and foredeck gang (and later, Ensenada marauders) while skipper Bob Grant, Ed Warmington, and Nacho Lozamo comprised the afterguard. I fell somewhere in between, being too infirm (recovering from a broken leg) to be foredeck and too ignorant to be afterguard. It was a good group. Bob, Ed, and Nacho had enough racing experience down the Baja coast so that racing to Ensenada contained few, if any surprises. Gerry, Larry, Taylor, and Norm all knew which

Robon's double-head rig slipped her quickly through the lee of Houston Snidow's 10-Meter *Braila*—our first significant conquest after passing an endless stream of smaller boats.

string to pull, when to pull it and how much.

Robon III was a shiny new Columbia 50 which lacked nothing in the way of racing (or cruising) equipment. She was the first of her class with a new single-piece interior molding which, besides providing beautifully clean and functional joinery, saved more than eight hundred pounds. As a result, Bob had Columbia fit a lead shoe to the bottom of the keel and increase the mast height and sail area. *Robon* carried a higher aspect ratio mainsail than a Standard Columbia 50 and a 150-percent double head rig comprised of a large overlapping genoa staysail and a high cut overlapping jib. While difficult to tack, and hard to fill in really light air, this rig appeared to work very well. We were never passed by a boat with a conventional genoa—including Bill Polly's highly touted Cal-37 *Conquest* and Gordon Curtis's sixty-two-foot S&S cutter *Naragansett,* among five hundred or so others.

At 1630 we ghosted past the Cal-40 *Argonaut. Simoon,* still astern, wiped off and set her mizzen staysail. She pulled abeam well to leeward, but she was forced to take the staysail down to maintain course. We were holding her once more. Unfortunately, this was not the last we were to see of *Simoon*'s effective mizzen laundry.

At 1720 we overhauled and passed *Conquest* with surprising ease, partly because she was stuck in the backwind of *Saluda,* the eighty-eight-foot scratch boat. *Saluda* was not enjoying the light going, and we made short work of her as well.

At 1830 we converged with the Kettenberg 41 *Tomboy.* We started to take her, but she managed to stay just ahead of our wind shadow. We had an equally difficult time with the Cal-40 *Tangent,* seesawing first ahead, then back in extreme slow motion.

The wind was failing—falling with the sun—and by nightfall we were almost completely becalmed off Mission Bay. For a while we made three knots through the water, but we weren't laying the course any more. Slowly, we ground in toward the beach near Point Loma.

Slowly is the word. Between 2300 and 0300 we made ten miles. On our watch between 0300 and 0700 we made even less. Since we were fairly close to the beach already, we felt that our only salvation lay in staying inshore. If there was a breeze offshore, those out there would be long gone. Besides, there was no way to get there.

We headed in for the beach with the ominous sound of the surf pounding on shore. At the first sign of kelp, we tacked—which killed all way—and sat, feeling dejected and sure all hope of a decent finish was lost.

While we had progressed not at all, dawn brought us the consoling sight of *Simoon* still astern and *Tomboy* and *Tangent* at least not ahead. The wind gradually returned with the daylight, and by 1030 it shifted to southwest and stared to fill in. I came on deck and looked forward for Point Loma. By George, it wasn't there, we had finally gotten past and had the Coronados in sight.

Sails started appearing from offshore as we drew abeam of the Coronados. Shortly after noon a spinnaker blossomed well to windward. Soon the wind had veered to the west and we were all beginning to boil along with chutes up. *Simoon* set her mizzen staysail and drew abeam but to windward. Our only hope was to stay low and not let her get on top of us. We tried desperately to hold her, but the wind continued to come aft. She set her mizzen spinnaker in place of the reaching staysail, and it was all over.

It was a grand sail in spite of *Simoon*'s disappearance. We were kept busy trying to fight off several Cal-40s and K-41s. By late afternoon we were dead before it, clicking off seven and eight knots, rolling down the Mexican coast. At 1745 we jibed for the finish, eight miles away. We were inside *Simoon,* but not enough to do any good. She finished eight minutes ahead of us to take Class A and the Mayor of Ensenada trophy.

Jack Bailley's *Newsboy* was first monohull to finish,

and she slipped into second place in Class A, but just barely. *Robon III* was a scant two minutes, seventeen seconds out of second place to take third in Class A.

Here we were in Ensenada about to find out why everybody came—and everybody did. Bob Grant describes it as the "Adults' Easter Week." At least one nonsailor drives to Ensenada for the festivities for every one who sails there. If five thousand sailors were there, the throngs on Ensenada's dusty streets numbered ten thousand. They jammed into bars, bought expensive souvenirs and cheap booze and carried on as if they'd been at sea for two months instead of a day and a half, or not at all.

Our foredeck gang attacked Ensenada but was repulsed after repeated sorties. The afterguard, to which I now attached myself for self-preservation, made a quick swing through town (on pretense of showing me around) before retiring early in preparation for an 0700 departure for San Diego. . . .

But not before the appearance out of the throng of the owner of a boat moored not one hundred yards from mine back in Connecticut.

"Hey, Frank Jewett!"

Gerry Grant launches his carrier pidgeon which he hopes will have sufficient endurance to take his message home to "Mom." It read: "I don't like baloney sandwiches. Love, Gerry."

IX

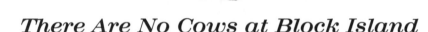

There Are No Cows at Block Island

BLOCK ISLAND HAS COW COVE on its north beach; it is the home of the legendary but extinct sailing fisherman known as the Cow Horn; and it has beautiful, rolling, rock-walled cow pastures—but no cows. In fact, there are no cows at Cowes, which is a roundabout way of saying that Block Island and the famous English port of Cowes, Isle of Wight, have much in common, if not cows: they both play host to spectacular race weeks.

Anyway, it all started at the Isle of Wight where Cowes Week, with its origins in yachting antiquity, combines the best of sailboat racing around the buoys for large cruising boats and smaller one-designs, with socializing of a high order. This is the granddaddy of all race weeks.

Block Island Week, which has become the yachting spectacle on the U.S. East Coast, was patterned directly after Cowes Week; and in recognition of this, the Island Sailing Club of Cowes presented a tankard to be awarded for the best corrected time in a special race around Block Island.

It was 1963 when Jakob Isbrandtsen, then vice-commodore of the Storm Trysail Club and owner/skipper of the U.S. Admiral's Cup team yacht *Windrose,* so enjoyed Cowes Week that he brought it to Block Island. He and the

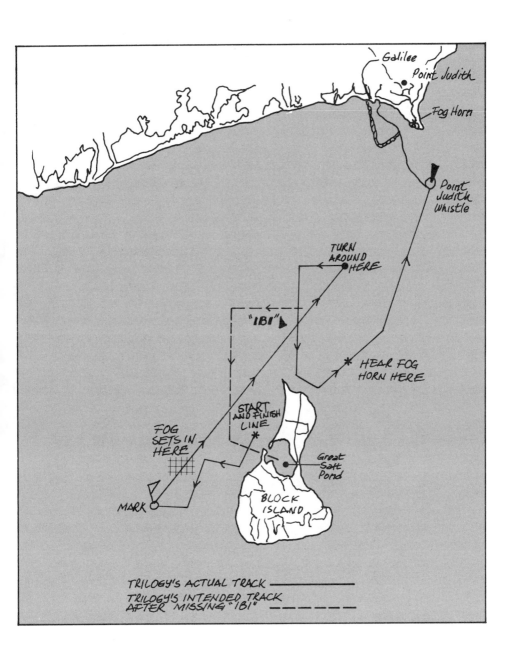

There Are No Cows At Block Island

late Ev Morris, yachting correspondent for the *New York Herald Tribune* and long-time sailor, conceived the Storm Trysail Club's Block Island Week and based it on the big-boat half of Cowes Week. The one-design people had their Larchmont and Marblehead race weeks, but there was no time or place for the big boats to gather in good weather and good fellowship for good racing. Block Island Week would fill the need. And so it has!

Block Island is a remote outpost of the state of Rhode Island. It lies about ten miles off the coast, has an excellent harbor called Great Salt Pond and is surrounded by deep, clean, blue water. "Block" is usually a mecca for unmarried schoolteachers, sportfishermen and cruisers (favored by both sail and power); but for a week in June on odd-numbered years it is taken over by offshore racing types.

Great Salt Pond can comfortably accommodate roughly two hundred boats. Invitations are limited to that number. Racing for most begins with feeder races from Long Island Sound, the South Shore of Long Island, and Narragansett and Buzzard Bays. These start Friday night or Saturday morning and are sponsored by local clubs rather than STC.

The week itself features fifteen- to twenty-mile races each day. Sometime during the week there is a lay day which may be used to make up canceled races. The feature event is the race around the island of about eighteen miles.

With contestants coming from such widely scattered areas as New Jersey and Maine, competition is bound to be at a high level, but the opening Block Island Week, in 1965, was something of a disappointment.

The first racecourse was from the start off the entrance to Great Salt Pond, to the Point Judith whistler—just about dead to windward in a light northerly—and return. Aboard Humphrey Simson's then new Gurney yawl *Kittiwake,* we had a nice port-end start and were

There Are No Cows At Block Island

going well, heading away from the island. Here we learned "Block Island Week Lesson Number 1": *Stay close to the island.* Those who tacked up the beach benefitted from a significant current boost (more significant than it would appear on the current charts) and were then treated to a nice lift as the wind veered northeast.

Kittiwake rode the lift, always pointing at Point Judith until we were approaching from the northwest. It was not our day.

It wasn't really anyone's day. The wind continued to be light and fluky, and the race was long and uninspiring even for those who were able to do well.

The balance of that first week produced either light air or dense fog. The racing was not good and mutterings of despair were heard that the STC should find a new week (the weather patterns were bad, it was said) or that would be the end of a good idea.

But everyone so genuinely enjoyed the activities both afloat and ashore in spite of the bad weather that the future success of Block Island Week was assured. It was decided subsequently that Block Island Week should be a biennial event.

We discovered aboard *Kittiwake* that a week of close racing around the buoys was worth a season of weekend overnighters. What a great way to tune and get more familiar with a new boat—or an old one, for that matter.

The first race two years later dispelled the theory that it never blows for BI Week. Having a moderate southwest wind at the start, the committee ordered the race around the island. They could have waited all summer for a better day than this one.

A short beat to the whistler off Southwest Point (all government marks are observed in the race around the island) produced a flurry of near collisions, actual collisions, groundings, and dismastings. There were just too many boats trying to get into too small an area near the beach south of the Great Salt Pond breakwater.

There Are No Cows At Block Island

After this was sorted out there followed a beam reach from the Southwest Point whistler in increasing wind. We aboard Bill King's thirty-two-footer *Drummer* were one of the first to set a chute, first to broach and definitely first to get it down. By the time we got to the run from Southeast Point past Old Harbor (which was after most had gotten there), the wind was fresh to strong and we were glad to be under wung-out genoa. Those with spinnakers still up either got them down smartly or gave the rest of us a show of broaching, jibe-broaching, and panic.

Fortunately, there were no special difficulties and everyone was soon under control—soon enough to be engulfed in a typical BI fog. With the wind still fresh, the fleet set off to find "1BI" off North Reef. Some, being either overeager or having optimistic DRs, found North Reef instead, but all got in sooner or later. Those getting in sooner were wildly enthusiastic, instant converts to Block Island Week racing. Those getting in later were only slightly less enthusiastic but also converted. We fell between the two.

Would that the balance of the week had gone as well. The weather cooperated with a good mixture of wind—mostly light, some medium from a variety of directions—but other events prevailed to start a BI Week tradition which will not, hopefully, be continued.

To give themselves a wider choice of courses, the STC committee made provisions for two temporary turning marks. On Tuesday, in light, drifting conditions and strong current, the STC divisions hit their mark so many times that it was reduced from a respectable tall buoy with STC burgee to an anchored life jacket. Some of the Class C and D boats found the latter hard to locate and grumbled disconsolately about it on into the night.

On Thursday some of the MORC division couldn't find their mark. A few did more than grumble, and formal protests were lodged against the race committee. These were disallowed, however, with unofficial but terse

There Are No Cows At Block Island

comments about the MORC division's navigators.

In spite of this, the second Block Island Week was declared an unparalleled success, and plans were begun immediately for a bigger and better one in 1969.

The third Block Island Week saw the biggest mark-missing protest of all time. The special marks (bigger and more substantial this time) again were set with a lead boat dispatched to spot them whenever they were in use. At the start of the third race the lead boat went to the mark, but it wasn't there. So the lead boat patrolled back and forth to find it. It so happened that the first leg was a broad reach with many contestants finding it difficult to keep down to the rhumb line as they scratched to windward in search of clear air. It also happened that the lead boat was searching two miles to windward of where the mark should have been when its skipper noticed that he was being chased by the leaders of the Class D (first class to use this mark). The lead boat quickly anchored where it was, and the fleet proceeded to round it.

This pretty well upset those who had held low only to find themselves chasing the fleet. Thirty protests were filed against the race committee. One was filed by the chairman of the protest committee, Ed Raymond, and one by another protest committee member. Several counter-protests were also filed in support of the race committee, but a special protest committee (empanelled to replace the two interested parties) upheld the thirty protests and threw out the race.

Two things happened as a result. The race committee said to hell with special marks (it was determined later that both had been stolen) and raced thereafter around the island, and Ed Raymond found himself appointed race committee chairman for 1971.

The racing in 1969 was better than ever once the STC got over the missing-mark problem. Winds were once again varied in strength and direction. The three races around the island were sailed in distinctly different wind patterns which offered a variety of racing even if there was no variety in course.

Thus the stage was set for late June every other year when about two hundred of the East Coast's offshore racers converge on Block Island to do battle with wind, current, and demon spirit.

Social activities on Block are fantastic. Free beer flows at the tent at Job's Hill, which is STC headquarters, and a Dixieland band plays continuously—at least as long as it is well lubricated. Block Island has some of the best seafood eating to be found on the East Coast. I prefer Deadeye Dicks, which belies its name and is served by nice grandmotherly-type waitresses instead of eye-patched pirates as one might expect.

Some prefer the more swinging atmosphere of Ballards over at Old Harbor. This is definitely the place for after-dinner things even if you don't eat there, which many people do.

Of course, each year brings something new and the action may well be at other places in other years, places like the Royal Hotel, Smuggler's Cove, or 76 Yellow Kittens.

In spite of the party atmosphere that prevails, or perhaps because of it, many people make it a family week. More than a few rent summer cottages, which are available in some quantity on the island, and bring the wife, kiddies, and even a babysitter. The STC encourages this by organizing island tours, skeet shoots, and other shore activities for the noncombatants.

There is plenty to see and do on Block. Even though it rained part of every day in 1969 and we had only the barest essentials aboard our twenty-four-foot modified Shark *Teazer,* my wife, two medium-sized sons and I never wished to be elsewhere. We managed a bicycle tour of the island on the lay day (no cows anywhere) and the kids easily consumed ten dollars worth of free soda and food which was the cost of their ID buttons. (Everybody needs one.)

There Are No Cows At Block Island

One learns very quickly how to play the wind and currents around the island when one does it every day for a week. Generally, it pays to stay close to the island because the wind is almost always stronger there. Playing the currents is important, too, and while the current chart is of such small scale as to be nearly useless, it will show the direction of flow. From there you're on your own.

There is a distinct shelf running around most of the island. This can be used to advantage—getting on the shelf in diminished current when it is against you, and riding the edge of the shelf in stronger current when it is favorable.

One must be careful of the many rock piles that dot the water near the island, but they are all well-marked on the detail chart. It is imperative to be both precise and courageous when playing the beach, which is done to most advantage along the west side of the island and around North Reef.

There is a passage through North Reef for boats drawing less than five feet. In light air and strong current conditions, this passage is clearly defined by the absence of a tide rip. If you run aground trying this don't say I told you to do it!

In a southwest wind the bluffs around Southeast Light tend to slow the wind near the beach. This affect can be felt as much as a mile offshore, so don't hug the beach here under these conditions. There are many mean rocks and wrecks along this beach anyway to discourage beach crawling.

The currents seem to be weaker on the east side of the island. I have never been able to observe any particular difference in current inshore or off on this side, but I have been blanketed behind Clay Head in a southwester. Again, stay off the beach here.

There are no hard-and-fast rules, only general ones, about racing near Block Island. The best possible advice is to use your head, do your navigating carefully and constantly (in case of sudden fog), and watch the boats ahead and behind for signs of good or bad places to be.

I cannot overstress the importance of good navigation. I have never had difficulty personally, although I have encountered some pretty frightful conditions, but two of the best racing skippers I know have tried to ride the radio beacon at Southeast Light and sailed right past the island.

Don't let this happen to you. There are no cows at Block Island so you can't home in on the cowbells. And if you sail right by, look at all the fun you'll be missing.

It is easy to be a prophet; all it takes is a little courage—or is it foolheartiness? In fact, I had sailed in the vicinity of Block Island for many years. My first visit was as a teenager aboard a powerboat—not that one learns much about sailboat racing aboard a powerboat—and I had since been to and from Block, around it in both directions, and even over it more times than can be remembered. I had seen it in calms, gales, sunshine, moonlight, starlight, cloudy skies, and dense fog. I had always been careful of my navigation, and while several of my friends and racing competitors had gone astray in Block's environs, I had not. To be sure there had been anxious moments, but they always had turned out as planned. I had split in two the narrow channel into Great Salt Pond after twenty miles of fog from Plum Gut. I had found "ıBI" in dense fog, and I had used the combination of wind and current to outwit a fleet of opponents. It was simply a matter of careful navigation—paying attention. No wonder I could write so cockily about the mysteries of Block Island sailing in the spring of 1971.

Comeuppance must eventually be the fate of the overconfident and the boastful. I received mine that very June. We had come to Block Island Week to win the MORC division, and except for my error in navigation we may very well have. Now that time has had its salutary effect, I can laugh at my own folly.

There Are No Cows At Block Island

Block Island Week began, for us, with two near disasters; the third—which undid us—was bound to happen. Tom Norton, the designer of *Trilogy* and my partner in her ownership, had sailed her to Block with his wife Barbara, my wife Dorcas, and my son Doug (age thirteen). Another son, Bill (age eleven), was with me aboard my Bertram 20 *Zap!*, which was to be our "mother ship" for the week. Unfortunately, we had been having trouble with *Zap!*. It didn't steer too well to port. Seeing us motor into the harbor, Tom brought *Trilogy* around and headed close aboard our starboard side—assuming we had normal maneuverability, and we very nearly collided amid much shouting and waving in the middle of Great Salt Pond.

Our second near-disaster occurred at the start of the first race. In our eagerness to do well, we started prematurely, and when we returned and crossed the line properly, we were almost last boat in the MORC class of fifty. We were not to be denied, however, and by a combination of good luck, cool helmsmanship, and skillful navigation, we were back up with the leaders by the time they reached 1BI. By Southeast Point only Skip Raymond's Tartan 30 was ahead of us. We were unable to save our time on Skip, but our second-place finish stood on corrected time. We had made a propitious beginning.

The second race found us in fifth place at the first (windward) mark. Skip Raymond was again in the lead but we felt we were well within our handicap on his boat and the other two with him. Those behind, to most of whom we owed time, were well back. With our continued luck we would finish far enough ahead to save our time.

As we crossed west of the entrance to Great Salt Pond, the ferry from Block to Newport headed out through the fleet, and we concentrated on projecting our respective course lines to avoid interference. At this crucial juncture, Dorcas and I traded jobs. She had been navigating on the windward leg, and I had been trimming the spinnaker after we rounded. Now Dorcas took over the spinnaker, and I went below to look at the chart. The fog, which had been threatening all morning, rolled over us.

I took some hasty bearings to obtain a fix and took over the navigation in earnest. We had been able to see 1BI before the fog obscured it, but the currents to the north of the island are very swift and erratic. What would have been an easy adjustment in the transition from the weak current adjacent to the island to the strong current off the north end of the island with good visibility became a complicated combination of geometry and guesswork in the thick fog. I spent the few miles left to 1BI moving from the chart table below to peering over the side looking for current rips attempting to second-guess my own navigation.

When we passed through a tide rip I assumed that we had not allowed sufficiently for the easterly set north of the island and were well over the reef marked by 1BI. I ordered what I considered was an appropriate adjustment in the course. I did not check the reef position with our estimated speed.

We sailed on this corrected course until our ETA (estimated time of arrival) ran out and continued for an additional two minutes when nothing was seen or heard of bell (1BI's sound characteristic) or other competitors. Naturally, I was quite upset that we had missed the mark. Lying fifth, close to the leaders, we would have had an excellent second race to go with our first race second place. It was imperative to find the mark *right now!*

I assumed that we had passed to the eastward of 1BI and, since we had exceeded our ETA, that we had sailed beyond it. We came hard on the wind on the port tack heading as high as possible or about due west. We took short hitches west and south but we saw and heard nothing.

One might think that all we had to do was be sure we had passed beyond the mark and then head for the finish line. However, the racing rules require that a competitor

There Are No Cows At Block Island

see a mark of the course—dead reckoning is not considered sufficient evidence of having rounded. We were honor-bound to find the mark or withdraw from the race.

After twenty minutes I began to realize that the race was lost and that we had better start thinking about finding Block. All on board started "hearing" bells, "seeing" lights, and conjuring up bell shapes in the fog. A few of the more positive of these caused momentary deviations in our planned course, but I do not believe that they were significant enough to cause our ultimate problem—our being totally disoriented.

We eventually sailed close to a yawl from one of the larger classes. They said they thought the island was to the north, and we followed along with them until we realized that they were just as confused as we were.

In desperation we gave up the race and I plotted a course from an assumed point near 1BI on the wind on the port tack. Laying out a half-hour leg on this course would put us well to the west of the north-south axis of the island. Then another half-hour starboard tack should take us to some point along the western shore of the island. If after an hour we did not intercept the island we would sail east until we ran into it (assuming we could see shore before going aground). We followed this pattern, and at the end of the second half-hour no beach appeared. I began to fear that we had sailed past the south side of the island, a groundswell characteristic of that area had appeared, but we couldn't hear the horn of Southeast Light—which should have been audible from that position.

During this time I had been attempting to plot radio bearings on Montauk, Point Judith, Brenton Reef, and Buzzards Bay. Unfortunately, I couldn't pick up Montauk or Point Judith, which would have provided east/west position information. The line of position I received from Buzzards Bay told me what I already knew, we were on a line passing near the north side of Block Island.

Then, at last, we heard a horn. It was a real horn, not

someone's imagination. We all heard it and heard it at the same time. We all even agreed on the direction from which it was coming. Could it be the horn at the entrance to Great Salt Pond? I dove below to consult the "Eldridge" pilot book, but the Great Salt Pond horn was not listed. As much as we had all listened to that horn, none of us could remember its characteristic. As we approached, heading north, we established a definite interval on the horn we were hearing at fifteen seconds. No such horn was listed on the chart anywhere near where I thought we were.

We headed for the horn for a long time. The children —who had been stalwart crew until now—began to appear concerned. Wives cast questioning glances at helmsman and navigator. Still, we had a definite objective— find the horn—and then we would know where we were.

Then we heard a whistle buoy and almost simultaneously sailed past a tall buoy with a blue flag. Both Tom and I recognized this as the type of lobster-pot marker used in Rhode Island Sound, and when we heard the whistler again we knew we were approaching Point Judith. A quick check on the chart confirmed Point Judith's horn characteristic as a fifteen-second interval, and the chart showed the Point Judith whistle buoy in a logical relationship to our present heading and the bearing to the sound of the horn.

By now it was getting late. Rather than head for Block Island for more groping around in fog and probably darkness, we continued in to Point Judith where we knew we could find a harbor, phone race headquarters to let them know we were okay (and forstall a search), and get some dinner.

We had a wonderful lobster dinner which everyone enjoyed except me. I'd rather have been eating a bologna sandwich in Great Salt Pond. I was thoroughly demoralized.

After dinner I phoned the Coast Guard to verify what we could see in Point Judith's Galilee harbor—the fog had lifted. We had a delightful starlit sail the eleven miles

There Are No Cows At Block Island

back to Great Salt Pond, or so I am told. I went below to sulk and go to sleep.

It was days before I could reconstruct what had gone wrong and where we had been while bumbling around in the fog. The key clue came from Skip Raymond (who had found the mark and gone on to win the race). Skip said he came upon the mark with eight minutes to go on his ETA. We had all underestimated the northerly set of the current. *Trilogy* had, in all probability, sailed two miles or more past the mark before turning back. Our "find Block Island" pattern had then put us scrambling around to the north and east of the island (into Cow Cove!) instead of south and west.

In retrospect I think we did the right things. None of us were really worried, and I never had the slightest doubt that we would get in safely. But when you've always been able to cope with whatever comes up, it is a very uncomfortable feeling not to be able to get where you want to go because you don't know where you are starting from. I was very unhappy.

We were, of course, the talk of Block Island. Lots had gotten lost—my oldest son BJ, sailing aboard *Destination,* ended up in Old Harbor on the east side of Block—but none had done so in quite as spectacular a fashion. We vindicated ourselves the next day by being the first boat in the fleet of two hundred ten to reach the weather mark, and we went on to win the race. However, with one race left in the series and a record of 2, DNF, 1 . . . nothing we could do in the last race could salvage the series.

Of course I was the butt of considerable good-natured derision following the unplanned trip to Point Judith and an article in the August 1971 issue of *One-Design & Offshore Yachtsman,* recounting the experience, amounted to a public confession. For more than a year it haunted me. I'd meet someone for the first time, and he'd say with a chuckle, "Oh, you're the guy who got lost in the fog. . . ." There was nothing to do but laugh along.

Then I received an invitation through Tom Norton to

sail the last day of the 1972 MORC Nationals at Stonington with Charlie Lea who had chartered *Trilogy* from us for the week. One of Charlie's crew had conflicting plans for the final day, and I was asked to take his place. *Trilogy* had not done well. She was a light-air boat, and it had been a very heavy weather series, but the final day dawned with perfect *Trilogy* conditions—very light.

Tom, who was skippering, made an excellent start. *Trilogy* was soon in the lead, moving away from the fleet. Only Joe Bartlett's Cal-28 was in a threatening position, and we were moving on them perceptibly. Our course was to Cerberus Shoal and return from a starting line just off the beach east of Watch Hill.

Navigating was Rick Stowe, a business associate of Charlie's. Rick had almost no previous experience, but he was very bright and had no trouble understanding the concepts. He went about his work in a thorough and confident manner, asking either Tom or me whenever he had a question—which was infrequently.

About three-quarters of the way to Cerberus Shoal we were enveloped by fog. Visibility was reduced to less than a mile. Sometimes it was only a hundred yards. The Cal-28 and all those behind her disappeared from sight.

We had been on port tack when the fog enveloped us —almost to the lay line for Cerberus. Rick indicated a certain amount of nervousness, but Tom and I assured him that if he stuck with his plot he could tell us when to tack for the mark. We tacked on Rick's cue and sailed to the Cerberus buoy as if tied to it by a string. We rounded triumphantly, set the spinnaker, and took up a reciprocal heading for the start/finish line.

When we were about halfway there, by Rick's calculations, we began to hear the horn at Watch Hill. It sounded dead ahead, but as we approached the unseen beach the sound seemed to come more and more from the west. This was as it should have been, and when the sound was coming from almost abeam we guessed we

There Are No Cows At Block Island

were very close to the beach.

The wind had been diminishing as we closed with the Rhode Island shore. Still, we didn't want to be caught in a panic situation with the spinnaker up and sand suddenly in sight a hundred yards or less away. We altered course very slightly, heading up under genoa as the spinnaker came down. We strained in vain to hear any sounds from the committee boat (as a vessel anchored in a fog in a fairway, they should have been sounding a bell), but we heard nothing.

Suddenly, there was the buoy marking one end of the line. We sailed close to it—looking for the committee boat without success—and when we were abeam of the buoy we recorded our time. Passes to the east and west failed to locate any sign of the race committee, so we anchored in position to form a finish line and waited for Joe Bartlett (or someone else) to find us. Seconds passed, then minutes, then our time on Joe expired, then our time on the rest of the fleet passed. We had won the race.

Half an hour after we had finished, the Cal-28 came in. We recorded his time and chatted about the weather and the race—receiving Joe's congratulations on our excellent navigation. Gradually, the rest of the fleet straggled in, and eventually the race committee—which had gone back to Stonington for lunch—found the finish line and relieved us.

Months later at the annual dinner of the New York MORC station, several people remarked that I had erased my Block Island Week error with a "brilliant piece of navigation" in the last race of the MORC Nationals. "It wasn't me," I corrected. "Rick Stowe was the navigator."

"That's okay," said one of my friends, "it was a brilliant piece of navigation anyway."

X

Zap! *and the Fogbound Baron*

I HAD BEEN COVERING THE America's Cup trials off Newport for much of the summer of 1970, and the day in question began much as others aboard my Bertram 20. I was headed for the starting line of what we all expected to be (and ultimately was) the last day of the series between the 12-Meters *France* and *Gretel II* to see which yacht would challenge for the America's Cup. Aboard with me was West Coast editor Chris Caswell, and lifetime America's Cupophile and Aussie, Bob Harris.

We had left the harbor earlier than usual for this series because the racing area for the challengers was well offshore—starting at the end of the torpedo range to the east of Block Island—to keep the challengers from interfering with the New York Yacht Club's course where the American Twelves were vying for the right to defend. Still, with the Bertram's speed we were able to leave well after most of the fleet had slipped past Fort Adams and on out into Rhode Island Sound.

She was ideal for my purposes that summer, which were to observe and photograph the America's Cup trials. With her 210 hp OMC sterndrive she would do an honest thirty-five knots (forty-two the book said, but maybe that was in new condition) which allowed me to zap from Connecticut to the racecourse in three hours, and zap

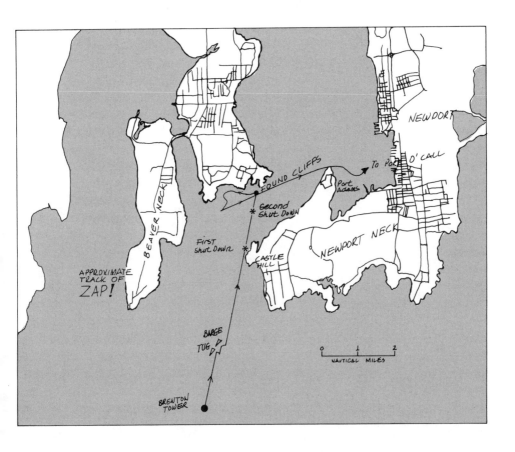

from the American Twelves to the Australian/French series in a couple of minutes to keep tabs on both. She was small enough, and left so little wake, that I could zap in close to the racers for a photograph and then zap out again without interfering. What else could I call her but *Zap!*? And *Zap!* we went out to the racecourse.

It had been one of those typically hazy Newport days, and minutes after the start of the race the two 12-Meters suddenly disappeared into a thick fogbank. The hodgepodge fleet of spectator craft that were following the racers couldn't cope. Skippers slowed down, stopped, turned this way or that trying to deal with the fog, trying not to interfere with the Twelves, trying not to run down a fellow spectator, and trying not to be run down themselves.

"This is no place for us," I told Chris and Bob. We wouldn't be able to see anything, and I didn't want to mingle with the milling throng. I suggested we make our way to the weather mark and sit it out there, waiting for the yachts to round.

It should have been easy to locate the mark since it was four miles directly to windward. However, we couldn't take the direct route without running the risk of interfering with the racers. My plan, which I hastily outlined for my shipmates, was to run three sides of a square pattern, departing from the starting area at ninety degrees off the heading to the weather mark. I knew from timed runs that *Zap!* would do twenty-five knots at 3500 rpm. It appeared we had sufficient visibility to go that fast, and with the distance to the weather mark being four nautical miles, at twenty-five knots it would take us ten minutes (9.6 actually) to get there were we able to go directly to it. By running for five minutes at ninety degrees off the heading to the first mark, turning to that heading for ten minutes to get us abeam of the mark, then turning the reciprocal of the first heading for five minutes, we should—in theory—come right to the weather mark. It would take us a total of twenty minutes, which should be plenty of time before the Twelves got there, and we should see them round. Chris and Bob shrugged agreement with my logic and settled down to be sharp lookouts. Off we went!

As *Zap!* settled into her stride we had the ocean to ourselves. An occasional lobster-pot buoy or low-flying seagull reassured us that we were not overspeeding our visibility. At exactly five minutes, I turned ninety degrees to port and punched the stopwatch again. At ten minutes we turned to port again, and I silently crossed my fingers. Fortunately, there was very little current in this area, the wind was light, and the seas were calm. At twenty-five knots none of these factors which one has to consider so carefully in a sailboat were significant. We would hit the mark right on the button.

At about two-and-a-half minutes I glanced off to port; and there, looming out of the fog, was the blue-hulled *France.* She was just about abeam, three hundred yards off. *Zap!*'s wake would catch her right on the bow! I cut the throttle (a futile gesture, the damage having already been done) and remonstrated with myself for being in the way. I had prided myself in never having interfered with a racing yacht while taking photographs, and here I was practically creating an international incident by cutting in front of Baron Marcel Bich's America's Cup contender.

But wait a minute. I shouldn't have been on the course at all, the way I set up the pattern. Maybe *my* navigation was correct. Maybe it was *France* who was having navigational difficulties. Ah well, there was nothing to do but resume our course after watching *France* pass and disappear once more into the fog.

Precisely two minutes and fifteen seconds later, the mark boat appeared ahead. We had arrived, as planned, at our destination along with a half-dozen others of the once large spectator fleet. A couple of minutes later *Gretel II* came out of the fog to leeward and rounded the mark to the salute of half-a-dozen spectators' horns. The Aussies set their spinnaker smartly and *Gretel* disappeared quickly in the direction of the reaching mark.

Where was *France?* We weren't saying.

Eventually she, too, found the mark and went off following in the wake of the Australians many minutes later.

Again, a conference with my shipmates was called for. Should we blunder off in search of the other marks or wait here for the yachts to return on their second round or until the fog lifted? In view of our hairy encounter with the Baron's *France,* I opted to wait. I got no objection from my crew.

The fog remained. The Aussies found the weather mark for the second time, and this time the French did also—apparently without a detour. During the interval between the first and second appearances of the 12-Meters the spectator fleet began to grow as one by one they groped their way through the fog. A few chose to try to follow the Twelves, but we remained since the finish would take place at this mark. After what turned out to be a disappointingly dull day, the inevitable procession drew to a close. As was a foregone conclusion all afternoon, the Australian crew found the finish line. They crossed to the traditional chorus of horns and whistles, and won the right to challenge for the America's Cup. The baron's grand gesture of that morning when he had stepped to the helm of *France* himself—resplendent in white yachting attire—was now a fiasco.

He was lost in the fog . . . *again.* (The history books will tell you the baron was lost in the fog only once that day.)

Of course, aboard *Zap!* and the other spectator boats, we couldn't know what had happened to *France*—that she would fail to find the finish line altogether and not make Newport until late that night. On the one hand it seemed polite to wait for *France* to finish. On the other hand it seemed prudent to get the hell out of there before

Zap! and the Fogbound Baron

the spectator fleet cluttered the course for Newport. Prudence won out over formalities. Bob and Chris had had enough sitting around and waiting, they said, and we *Zap!*ed out of there.

With the start at the torpedo-range buoy "A" and the finish line four miles about southwest from there, we were about fifteen miles south-southwest of Newport. We had to rely on the unknown precision of the race committee in setting the weather mark for accuracy of our point of departure, and we were stuck with a minimum of twenty knots cruising speed. At less than 3000 rpm I had no idea how fast *Zap!* would go off plane, and it was essential to know precisely. Would the fog provide enough visibility for us to go twenty knots safely? I surely hoped so. The alternative was to mush along at uncertain speed, yet I had no desire to tangle with a lobster pot, another boat, or one of the spidery legs of Brenton Reef Tower, our intermediate mark outside of Narragansett Bay. Fortunately, there were enough lobster-pot buoys with nicely visible dark blue flags looming out of the fog to give us the estimated assurance that we could stop in time to avoid any unforeseen obstacles.

We didn't know it, but there were to be a couple of unforeseen obstacles. Shortly after settling down for the long, tedious run to Brenton Reef we encountered the first. It was *France!* Again we crossed the baron's bow, and again we threw our wake into a yacht racing in an international event. However, we didn't give it much thought this time—the series had been decided. We didn't even slow down, pretending we didn't see, acting as one might ashore when suddenly one spies someone across the street whom one doesn't want to see.

We ran out our estimated time of arrival to Brenton Tower, but there was nothing in sight and no horn could be heard. I shut down the engine. Sure enough, the foghorn blasted loudly just off to starboard. So far, so good.

"Look," I said to my crew, "I want to see that thing

and know just exactly where we are before we go off after Castle Hill" (the little lighthouse on Newport Neck where I planned our landfall). Motoring very slowly toward the direction from which the sound of the foghorn came, it seemed we would never get there. Suddenly, Chris shouted, "Up there!" and pointed his arm up at a forty-five-degree angle. Sure enough, there was the body of the tower high above us. Only after we had seen it could we make out the water surging around the legs, and then the legs themselves. I swallowed my heart realizing that my adrenal glands had been pumping furiously.

We had come this far, but we were far from safety yet. The visibility was down now. We were marginally safe, at best, going twenty knots and being able to see maybe seventy-five yards. Our landfall was a rocky coast, and Brenton Reef juts well out into the ocean to the east of the entrance to Narragansett Bay. I didn't want to head for the buoy that marked it for fear of going past it onto the reef. Castle Hill, with its mechanical bell, would be a better bet, and there was a bell buoy marking Butter Ball Rock just before Castle Hill. There was good water right up to the rocks, providing us with maximum stopping time should we suddenly come upon them, and the shoreline angled in from the east, providing us with a gradual shelf on that side. Should we be too far west and miss Castle Hill, we should be able to hear either bell when abeam of them. It seemed like the best approach.

With just a hair over two miles from Brenton Reef Tower to Butter Ball Rock buoy, I figured we would shut down after six minutes and listen for the bell if we hadn't seen anything by then. After double-checking the course and rechecking the stopwatch, I eased the throttle forward once again and let it settle down to 3000 rpm.

No sooner had we left Brenton Tower than we heard another foghorn. To me the sound of an unexpected foghorn in a thick fog is just about the scariest thing in the world. I imagine the *Q.E. II,* at least, and maybe the *An-*

drea Doria and the *Flying Dutchman* as well. However, this one had a pattern to it—a long and two shorts—a tug with a tow. At least it was not a U.S. Navy cruiser coming out of the bay at twenty knots for a combined closing speed of forty! We answered the signal with our Freon horn when we heard it again, and kept on going.

Almost exactly three minutes later, with the tug's foghorn getting louder all the time, its dark bow popped out of the fog. The band of white foam below the baggy-wrinkle fender looked like froth in the whiskers of a mad dog. It was heart-in-mouth time again! I turned hard to starboard (east) and chopped the throttle as soon as I could see we were safely out of the tug's path; stop the watch, swallow heart, advance throttle, turn back on course, start watch. Pfew!

Now I learned something that I should have realized long before. When a tug pulls a blunt-bowed barge, the barge doesn't necessarily follow dutifully directly behind the tug. Rather, it surges from one side to the other. Suddenly, there was the barge, its bow wave a great line of white water extending from one limited horizon to the other. Again I turned hard to starboard, again I chopped the throttle when we were out of the barge's path, stopped the watch, swallowed my heart, etc., etc.

This was the worst possible place to have an interruption in course or speed or timing, however slight. But there was no help for it. Easing the throttle forward, restarting the watch, I headed—badly shaken—for what I could only hope would be a friendly landfall instead of a rending crash. We ran out our six minutes, shut down, and listened.

Silence!

"Okay, Jones, what now?" were the unspoken questions of my anxious shipmates. "We'll go another thirty seconds," I said, remembering that the distance was a bit over two miles. Throttle forward, start watch, look out carefully, time elapsed, shut down, listen. . . .

Silence!

About fifteen seconds of the second thirty-second run had elapsed when I noticed a subtle change in the surface of the water. As I reached for the throttle, there came the cry "Rocks!" It was Chris again, this time echoed by Bob Harris's "Jeesus Keerist!" I saw it too: a wall of rock extending from the water up to our restricted infinity, and this time the breaking water *did* extend from horizon to horizon. I jammed the throttle back so hard that the sterndrive's lifting motor was overpowered. The drive unit tilted up and the propeller thrashed ineffectively in reverse, half in and half out of water. The exhaust note, no longer muffled by the water, sounded ten times louder as it reverberated off the cliffs ahead. It seemed to take forever for *Zap!* to shudder to a halt. When she finally did, we couldn't have been more than a boatlength from the breaking water at the base of the cliff.

One problem was solved—we had found land, and whatever happened I was not going to lose sight of it. One problem remained, however: Where were we?

The rocks we could see didn't give us a clue. They didn't look anything like those I had seen on Castle Hill. Still, where could we be? Thinking back on our two turns toward the east when we encountered the tug and barge, I surmised that we had somehow sneaked in behind Brenton Reef, and I tried desperately to remember what the shoreline looked like just east of Castle Hill. I couldn't.

Faced with a choice of turning east or west, I chose west, and we paralleled the cliff as far off as we could get and still see it. Moving now at virtually drifting speed, we all looked ahead in the water for signs of submerged reefs while I kept us within sight of the cliff and watched the compass. It started turning toward the north. Good! We kept going. Then, to my amazement, the compass turned west again, then *south!* This didn't make any sense to my confused brain.

"What in the hell is going on?" I asked aloud. All I got

back were dumb stares that said, again unspoken but plain enough, "What have you gotten us into, Jones, you're going to kill us all!"

Then, out of the fog to seaward, Bob spotted a buoy. "Thank God! Something to tell us where we are!" There was breaking water between us and the buoy, but we skirted gingerly around that and approached until we could identify it as gong "7" off Southwest Point on Conanicut Island. We had missed Castle Hill altogether (I found out later that the mechanical bell was no longer in operation) and fetched up in a rock-studded cove just east of Southwest Point.

From here on it was no sweat. I set a course for bell "11" off Bull Point. We passed gong "9" just where it should have been, and then we burst out of the fog onto a beautiful, sunlit Newport. Fort Adams and Goat Island looked absolutely wonderful. We tied *Zap!* to her slip and staggered weakly ashore and to the Black Pearl for a much-needed and well-deserved Mount Gay and tonic. We not only had made it in, we were the first to reach shore with the news that the Aussies had won and the baron was lost in the fog.

XI

The Saint Petersburg to Fort Lauderdale Race

BEFORE FIDEL CASTRO'S revolution in Cuba, there was an ocean race from Saint Petersburg to Havana. I have heard many tales of the splendid time everyone had in Havana after they got there, but no one ever mentions what kind of ocean race it was. I never made it, so I missed the night life in Havana—which seemed to be the biggest reason for the race.

What replaced the Havana Race in the Southern Ocean Racing Conference calendar in 1961 was a race from Saint Petersburg to Fort Lauderdale. First reports on this race from those used to racing to Havana were quite derogatory. It was a race from nowhere to nowhere in the minds of many. Who would want to end up in *Fort Lauderdale* after sailing nearly four hundred miles? And *Saint Pete,* there is only one reason to go there and that is to go on the Havana Race—or so the arguments went. It's too cold in Saint Pete. There's nothing to do there. There aren't any facilities for servicing ocean racers. There's nothing there but old people. And so forth.

It was yacht designer and international ocean racer, Dick Carter, who first spotted the Saint Peter-Fort Lauderdale Race for what it was instead of where it went. Following the 1966 race, Dick called it one of the finest ocean races in the world, and while he hadn't done all the

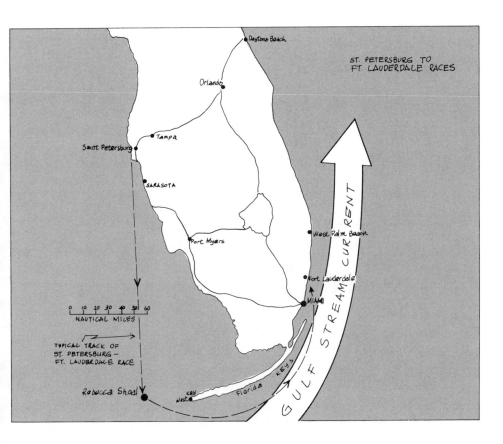

Saint Petersburg to Fort Lauderdale

world's ocean races he had surely sailed enough to be able to qualify as a judge. Uninterested in whether a race went from "somewhere to somewhere" or not, what Dick saw was a technically interesting and extremely challenging course with a variety of weather and sea conditions. All the skills of ocean racing are tested in this race, and luck plays a minimal part.

The beginning of this race, which has traditionally started off the Municipal Pier at Saint Pete, is less than ideal. As a matter of principle, an ocean race should start and finish in the ocean, and this one has (except for the 1978 SORC when it started outside the Sunshine Skyway in open water) always begun in the shallow, restricted waters of lower Tampa Bay. From there on, however, the course is perfect.

Once out of Tampa Bay, the course turns south toward Rebecca Shoal, an extension of the coral-reef system which forms the Florida Keys. Rebecca is approximately one hundred eighty miles south from Tampa Bay and forty-five miles west of Key West. This is a logical mid-point in the race. Normally this leg will be sailed in strong northerly winds—making it a surfing run—or in light to moderate west or southwesterly winds—making it a beat or close reach. From Rebecca one has to decide whether or not to head out to intercept the Gulf Stream to take advantage of its current, which can add two or three knots to a yacht's speed up the coast toward Lauderdale. The axis of the Stream on average is approximately fifty miles off Rebecca, and it would normally not pay to sail directly out to it. However, the Stream converges with the Keys, and another fifty miles up the coast it is quite close inshore and at its maximum velocity. One gets into the Stream eventually whether one wants to or not. The decision, then, depends very much upon the wind conditions one can expect from Rebecca onward; at what angle do you intercept the Stream?

One expects the Gulf Stream to be rough and one is

Saint Petersburg to Fort Lauderdale

seldom disappointed. The Gulf of Mexico can also be very rough in certain conditions. The water is relatively shallow—from thirty feet deep off Longboat Key to one hundred eighty feet deep near Rebecca—and in strong winds the seas can be steep and close together, giving boats an extremely uncomfortable motion.

The combination of characteristics of the waters through which this race is sailed bring together most, if not all, of the skills a crew needs to win an ocean race. The winds are usually true and predictable, currents are usually predictable and play a major role in race strategy, weather forecasting is reliable, and conditions can range from very light to survival. Protracted calms are rare. Rough seas are the norm.

My first Saint Petersburg to Fort Lauderdale Race was in 1966 aboard *Kittiwake,* which has been referred to in previous chapters.

Over the years I have come to know Saint Petersburg as a pleasant town not entirely deserving of its reputation as solely a place old Northerners go to die. However, the morning before the 1966 Lauderdale Race (what they call it in Saint Pete) *Kittiwake*'s crew met at the Ponce de Leon Hotel's coffee shop for breakfast, and we were treated to a scene which reinforced the image. While waiting for our order we noticed a particularly old and frail-looking woman moving very slowly, hobbling on a cane toward the cashier. She looked like the stereotypic Saint Petersburg resident, but we were in for a surprise. As she reached the cashier's desk she turned—very slowly and with considerable effort—and said, "Coming, Mother?"

The account of the '66 race, which appeared in the April issue of *One-Design & Offshore Yachtsman* that year, tells the story. It was after this race that Dick Carter, sailing aboard Ted Hood's *Robin*—the Class C winner—made his observation that this was one of the world's great ocean races. Having made many more Lauderdale

Races as well as many others, I would remove the qualifying "one of." This may be the world's "best" ocean race.

ROUGH RIDE TO THE GOLD COAST

It was the kind of night that makes you ask yourself what in the devil you're doing there. You'd give just about anything to be doing something other than pounding—bang-bang-bang—for an infinite length of time into an infinite succession of waves.

We were beating into a thirty-knot wind that had been blowing from the south-southeast for two days and a half. With less than thirty fathoms of water under us, the seas were short, steep, and nasty; we couldn't see them, but we could feel them and taste the salt as the spray splashed at our faces.

I quietly cursed those responsible for my sudden presence in the Gulf of Mexico. I had planned to go skiing that weekend, but Skip Mansfield was ill and Alan Gurney, *Kittiwake*'s designer, had a deadline to meet. *Kittiwake* needed a warm body, and the boss graciously "gave me leave" to go. At the moment, Mansfield, Gurney, and boss were at the head of my hate list. I was soft and out of shape (skiing doesn't do much to toughen the hands and strengthen the arms) and generally unprepared for the incessant beating *Kittiwake* was handing me. It might be cold in Vermont, but at least my bed up there would have been warm, dry, and standing still.

Even before we left the dock, things did not go well. *Kittiwake* looked like a hospital ship. The skipper was complaining of strep-throat symptoms. Bob Derecktor had a severe case of the flu and was further subdued by a liberal dose of sulfa drugs. And now, half the crew was seasick—one for the second time in his life (the first time occurred twenty years previously in the same waters). One of my watch-mates dislocated his shoulder, and Bill

Saint Petersburg to Fort Lauderdale

Heine's locker filled with water which soaked his four-day supply of cigars (how to take the heart out of a fighting man). Only Seth Hiller remained untouched by our difficulties. When he wasn't maintaining his stalwart deck watch, he was strapped to the galley stove preparing a vital bowl of stew.

Another blow hit us at the start. We were early. Right on the line at the gun, we were with Don McNamara's Luders yawl *Tara* and Scrubby Wellman's Hood yawl *Indigo.* There were two recalls and *Tara* turned back immediately. *Indigo* appeared to be ahead of us so we held on expecting her to go back.

After about five minutes a patrol boat came alongside to tell us we were recalled. We jibed around and were the last boat of the last class to start. We had the whole fleet to catch and had just given away fifteen minutes besides.

We were heartened—somewhat—as we passed several boats on the beat out of Tampa Bay. Not only were we catching the smaller fry, but we overhauled and passed classmates *Nathaniel Bowditch* and *Marluva* and went under the Sunshine Skyway Bridge just astern of *Indigo* and *Touché.*

As midnight approached we slogged under Number-three genoa and a deeply reefed main, heading within fifteen degrees of the rhumb-line course on the port tack. There was no relief from the wild bucking as *Kittiwake* leaped from one sea to the next. She was moving well, though, as we overhauled and passed one set of running lights after another—all unidentified in the dark. Most of us were too miserable to feel much elation, but we hung on stubbornly and kept her driving. There wasn't much choice.

The forecast was for the wind to veer to the northwest with the passage of an advancing cold front. It would be accompanied by thunderstorms and winds to forty knots. Our strategy was to stay on the port tack until we were headed enough to favor the other tack. It was a fairly

Saint Petersburg to Fort Lauderdale

obvious plan, with lightning already visible to the west and north.

The wind started around ahead of the front, and we flipped at about three o'clock Sunday morning. The promised thunderstorm contained plenty of rain but little wind. There was a momentary panic-party on deck while the watch tried to decide if it was going to blow or not. But we were soon freed up and reaching toward Rebecca Shoal in a moderate northwester. The leftover slop from the southerly wind was still with us; the resulting confused sea was even more vicious than before.

At dawn we spotted a sloop ahead which we tentatively identified as the Tripp-designed Mercer 44 *Jolie Madame*. This revelation did not please Chuck Blair who had two bottles of Scotch bet with *Jolie*'s skipper, Jack Price. Just before sunset the previous day, Chuck had notable success at *Kittiwake*'s helm sailing through *Jolie Madame* to windward. The rest of us had been unable to accomplish the same feat, and we attributed Chuck's success to an insatiable thirst. Now, blast it, *Jolie* was ahead of us again. The only thing to do was to put Chuck back on the helm. He looked greatly determined, salivated slightly, and sure enough we started to close the distance.

As the wind hauled aft we were unable to stay with the sloop, so we hardened up ten degrees and with spinnaker and mizzen staysail drawing better we were definitely going faster. Unfortunately, we were again headed west of south, toward Dry Tortugas, and we didn't want to go there. We gradually worked up abeam and to windward of *Jolie*.

Now it was apparent, however, that the boat we thought to be *Jolie Madame* was instead one of the Lapworth-designed Cal-40s (we couldn't tell which of the two). Everyone was discouraged but Chuck—he was elated at the thought that his Scotch might still be won.

The trouble was that we gave the Cal-40 almost an hour and *Jolie Madame* only fifteen minutes. As night

Saint Petersburg to Fort Lauderdale

approached we pulled out to the westward and finally lost sight of the boat that had spurred us on for many hours. We were to meet again.

When we made our landfall at Dry Tortugas we were well west and south of our DR. The wind had veered to the east, and we had to take a hitch to get around the islands. We viewed this turn of events as a moderate disaster because it meant retracing our course to the *north* for several minutes.

Dawn, Monday, found *Kittiwake* past Rebecca Shoal, after an uneventful night, close-reaching into a light easterly and heading for the favorable current of the Gulf Stream. *Tara* was in sight just ahead. (We were well within our substantial time allowance). Astern was *Firebrand*, a 1965 Sparkman & Stephens design, built in England under the RORC rule for Dennis Miller, scratch boat in Class B.

Two miles dead to leeward was a yawl, and just visible on the horizon ahead was another. Careful scrutiny of the one to leeward revealed her to be *Big Toy*. We could hardly believe it. She is seventy-three feet overall and second from scratch in the fleet. By a process of elimination we determined that the yawl ahead was the sixty-three-foot Morgan-designed *Maredea*. Hot dog! We were well within our time allowance of *Maredea*—and no Cal-40 in sight. We were the hottest Class A boat around and had only to lose *Firebrand* to be in (apparently) excellent fleet position.

Losing *Firebrand* was not that easy. Then as the wind died away to zephyrs, a white dot appeared astern of *Big Toy*. The white dot became a sloop, the sloop became a Cal-40, and the Cal-40 became Ted Turner's *Vamp X* as she slid alongside and right by. She was our companion from the day before, except this time we could do nothing but try to hang on.

It was that way until the finish. The easterly freshened, and we romped up the Gulf Stream making seven

Saint Petersburg to Fort Lauderdale

knots through the water and almost three more over the bottom. A last desperate effort to shake *Vamp X* and *Firebrand* by holding out into the Stream succeeded only in costing us an additional fifteen minutes. We carried on too far and had to run, by the lee at times, the last few miles to the finish.

It's surprising how rapidly one's outlook can change. We had gone from glum depression to wild elation on finding ourselves in good position. It was a pleasant race after all. The skipper's strep throat had vanished; Bob Derecktor had beaten his sulfa drugs and flu into submission, and his normal oxenlike strength had returned. The dislocated shoulder was on the mend; Chuck was chuckling at the thought of drinking Jack Price's Scotch; I was ready to say to hell with skiing and admit that winter sailing was pretty good after all. Even Bill Heine couldn't have cared less whether he had a cigar or not. And Seth? He was in the galley preparing a celebration.

When the excitement had died down and the stragglers came in, the usual post-mortems revealed a clear pattern of the race. Those who were able to drive through Saturday night's hard going gained an initial advantage which helped them through the major turning point—getting around Rebecca Shoal before the calm. While everyone was becalmed for roughly the same length of time, the leaders were drifting toward Fort Lauderdale on the one- to two-knot Gulf Stream current. The smaller boats near *Rebecca* were caught in a northerly set for several hours, drifting the wrong way, their chances ruined for a good finish.

Several boats had difficulties with Saturday night's blow. *Otseketa* was dismasted. *Stiletto,* skippered by Ed Osborne, lost a headstay and returned to Saint Petersburg under power where she made hasty repairs and set out again. She was not counted as a finisher. *Escapade,* scratch boat in the fleet, broke her mizzen gooseneck and her triatic stay. Several boats blew out sails, including

Saint Petersburg to Fort Lauderdale

Tara who also broke her steering cable later in the Gulf Stream. In all, ten boats did not finish.

The "what if" faction says if Saturday night's front had held off, the big-boys would have gotten too far west while the little-fellows would have hit it just right. And if everyone had been out in the Stream when the wind quit, the Class C boats would have taken all the marbles.

It didn't happen that way, though it might next time. The little boats took a beating except for Ted Hood's *Robin Too* which won Class C. She came in 6 1/2 hours ahead of the next boat in her class and knocked us out of third in the fleet by twelve minutes.

I raced to Fort Lauderdale in 1969 with Charlie Morgan aboard his specially built Morgan 33, *outRAGEous.* This was a small boat aboard which to do a Lauderdale Race. It was very uncomfortable, but we survived and finished second in our class. The race was written up in the April issue of *O-D&OY* that year* and excerpts also appeared in *The Offshore Racer.*† It does not warrant being done a third time except to comment briefly on two highlights.

One of the toughest problems to cope with on so small a boat on so long a race is feeding the crew. You must eat to keep going. Normally one would add to "must eat", " ... and eat *well,*" but this didn't apply to this trip. Our plan had been to have sandwiches that could be gotten out of the icebox whenever anyone felt the need. However, Sam Cary—who had been delegated to obtain the sandwiches—realized after we had started the race that he had forgotten them; they were home in his refrigerator. This was not a crucial oversight. We had plenty aboard to eat, but most of the food required preparation.

---

*Ted Jones, "Rage? No, outRAGEous. Outrageous!" *One-Design & Offshore Yachtsman,* vol. 8, no. 4 (April 1969), pp. 51, 71.
†Theodore A. Jones, *The Offshore Racer,* op, cit pp. 220–24.

On a rough race in a small boat none of us was interested in cooking—even heating canned stew or spaghetti. We had two boxes of fried chicken, and Laura Morgan had given us a shoe-box full of brownies. Selfishly, I consumed most of the brownies. Every time I got hungry I'd go below, grab a handful of brownies and a Pepsi-Cola, and that would be my meal. I survived. Some of my seasick shipmates wished they wouldn't survive, but we all did.

At the time it didn't seem politic to mention another worry since Morgan was currently marketing the 33. Now, however, it's just an amusing anecdote. When we had turned Rebecca and were sailing on the wind in the Gulf Stream, *outRAGEous* would shudder and make the most unusual sounds. Each time we'd slam into a wave, a rapid-fire "boom, boom, boom, boom . . ." would come from the hull. *OutRAGEous* was not a stock 33 from the production line, and Charlie explained that in addition to the special interior (which was obvious) he had left out one layer of fiberglass in the hull layup. It was disconcerting, to say the least, to be sitting on deck bouncing over the seas with the "boom, boom, boom," while Charlie and Bruce Bidwell, his production manager, discussed whether or not it had been advisable to reduce the hull thickness. Ultimately, I was to gain great respect for this boat before the SORC was over, and she went on to sail under other owners after Charlie sold her. For all I know she is still going strong.

LOSING THE RUDDDER

For the 1970 SORC I was asked to be a part of the crew racing the first of a new line of boats—the C&C 35 *Redhead.* Bruce Kirby, editor of *O-D&OY,* was to be the skipper; George Cassian and George Cuthbertson, the designers, were to alternate races; George Hinterholler, the

Conditions were not ideal aboard *outRAGEous* for cooking which made it a critical oversight that Sam Carey had left the sandwiches ashore. Laura Morgan's brownies saved the day.

builder, was to do some races; and Ed Botterell, the sailmaker, would do them all. I felt in good company—especially in the thumping beat from the Boca Grande sea buoy to Venice in conditions which saw the wind speed at thirty-five (knots) exceed the air temperature at thirty (degrees Fahrenheit)—having designer, builder, and sailmaker for shipmates.

The start of the Saint Pete-Lauderdale Race was much like the race a few days previously to Venice—strong winds from the north-northeast which sent us hurtling down the Gulf toward Rebecca. *Redhead* was a relatively light boat for that time, and she really flew. We had control problems, however, and we were continually rounding up into semi-controlled broaches. It was on this leg that we learned how to keep the spinnaker flying (many of our competitors with similar problems had taken theirs down) to maintain speed while minimizing the risks of the inevitable and frequent broaches. The technique involved flying a reaching staysail which was overtrimmed under the spinnaker. Then, when the helmsman felt the spinnaker take charge, he would center the wheel—keeping as much speed on the boat as possible while making no further attempt to prevent the broach. *Redhead* would round up collapsing her spinnaker at which point she would come more nearly upright allowing the rudder to become effective in heading her off again. The staysail served to add driving force once the spinnaker had collapsed, and this sail area well forward assisted the helmsman in turning the bow away from the wind.

We must have been a spectacular sight, roaring along for six or seven waves, surfing past our more timid competitors until we'd round up in a wild broach. However, instead of lying on her side, *Redhead* would right herself, bear away, and leap forward again as her spinnaker filled with a pop. Our net speed was much greater than that of those too timid to set spinnakers, but the continual strain

Saint Petersburg to Fort Lauderdale

on the rudder proved to be too much.

Approaching Rebecca Shoal I was asleep below. Suddenly, I found myself on the cabin sole having been rudely dumped out of my bunk. *Redhead* was rolling uncontrollably, first rounding up, then bearing away and jibing. I looked up through the companionway to see Ed Botterell spinning the wheel frantically, then Bruce Kirby was there with the emergency tiller (which had been stowed under my bunk and explained why I was on the cabin sole), and I watched the wheel spin in conjunction with Bruce's frantic movements of the tiller. Still *Redhead* refused to respond.

I joined the others on deck, and helped take down the spinnaker. It wasn't until Lars Bergstrom leaned over the stern pulpit and announced in his lilting Swedish accent, "De rudder is gone!" that we knew what was wrong. No wonder the emergency tiller had no effect.

Clearly this was the end of the race for us. We were about five miles north of Rebecca Shoal—Key West, the nearest port. Joe McBrien, our navigator, radioed Homer Denius's sport fisherman *Stud Duck,* which was recording the roundings at Rebecca, that we were in difficulty, and Denius radioed back that he would come to our assistance after the last boat had rounded. We set about attempting to get *Redhead* under control.

Our first thought was to make an emergency rudder using the spinnaker pole. I drilled some holes in one of the bunk bottom-locker panels and bound this to one end of the spinnaker pole with seizing wire. Since it was my concoction, I got to try it out, and I was very nearly pitched over the side when I lowered the "blade" into the water and attempted to steer with it. The seas were too rough, and it was apparent that this rig would tear out the stern pulpit even if we succeeded in lashing it into position. (It proved useful later, maneuvering under power in the sheltered water of Key West harbor.)

Next we thought that some sort of drogue would hold

Redhead's stern into the wind and at least allow us to sail downwind under some control. The best idea seemed to be towing the bosun's chair astern. I shackled the light Danforth anchor to the bottom of the chair to hold it down, and we dropped it over the side on the end of the anchor line. It worked. *Redhead* came around before the wind, and we were able to set the number-four genoa. With this rig we sailed at about two knots before the twenty-five-knot wind, and soon we had Rebecca Shoal in sight.

We discovered that by rigging a bridle so that the pull of the bosun's chair would be directed from one quarter or the other, we could control direction within about twenty degrees either side of dead downwind. Rounding Rebecca we set the mainsail— reefed down—and by adjusting the main and jib sheets and the bridle we could sail at any point up to a close reach. We maintained our course on a beam reach at about four knots.

We debated whether or not we could reach Miami under this rig or even possibly finish the race. Our conclusion was that it would be possible but rather pointless. We would surely be a very distant last, and would be exposing ourselves to the possibility of stormy conditions which we might not be able to cope with. It was not worth the risk with assistance close at hand.

Stud Duck was soon alongside, offering us a tow, and we gladly accepted. Later we were to rendezvouz with a U.S. Coast Guard forty-footer which was to tow us to Key West. However, this was not the end of our difficulties.

It was late afternoon before the Coast Guard relieved *Stud Duck* of her burden, and soon we were bounding along in total darkness. Even though we were now the Coast Guard's responsibility, Joe McBrien—always the thorough navigator—kept track of our position.

There was something drastically wrong. Joe radioed the cutter that he was off course—that his proper course should be 065 degrees instead of almost 045 which we

Saint Petersburg to Fort Lauderdale

were heading. The Coast Guard, not about to take advice from someone they were rescuing, insisted that they were heading 065. McBrien fumed. It was apparent to Joe that our present heading would take us onto the reef into shallow water. Again he pleaded with the cutter, pointing out that we drew over five feet of water, and again he was rebuffed.

A short time later there was a loud thump, and *Redhead* shuddered as her keel bounced into the coral. "Boom, boom, boom," we hit repeatedly, unable to stop or turn away, being pulled irresistibly forward at the end of the towline. Joe dove for the radio while others ran forward to cast off the tow. The cutter's crew had felt the jerks, and stopped before we could drop the line. Canadian Joe, with a few choice words for the "U.S. Bloody Coast Guard" finally got their attention. They pulled us off into deeper water, and after several minutes of suspenseful silence the Coast Guard came back to us over the radio. "I'm sorry, Skipper," the voice said, "we put down a pair of pliers next to our compass. We're okay now, sorry."

Sputtering and muttering about incompetence, McBrien stomped about the cabin periodically checking to make sure we were not led astray again. I was the only U.S. citizen among the crew, the rest being Canadians, except for Lars. "You and your (expletive deleted) Coast Guard," Joe ranted, pointing at me. I had nothing to say in their defense, but we did make it into Key West without further incident.

Inspection the next day revealed that the rudder post had snapped off just below the hull. George Cuthbertson took the remaining part back to Toronto with him, and a new rudder—with a solid stainless-steel post—was flown down to Key West later in the week. *Redhead*'s captain Art Cook and Lars installed it and sailed her up to Miami. Meanwhile, we spent an afternoon and evening exploring Key West and then the rest of us flew home from

Marathon. Our chances for a place in the SORC were finished, but we would still be trying to finish well in the remaining races.

MOLASSES ON MOLASSES REEF

In 1972 I sailed once again with Humphrey Simson aboard a new Alan Gurney forty-eight-footer built by Palmer Johnson in Sturgeon Bay, Wisconsin. This was an uneventful race compared to other Saint Petersburg-Fort Lauderdale races I had sailed—particularly the previous one. Though only one foot longer overall, the new *Kittiwake* was effectively much bigger and more comfortable, and I don't think we even had spray on deck. We had some minor steering difficulty reaching down the Gulf of Mexico during which I clung to the emergency tiller for about twenty minutes while Alan crawled below to take slack out of the stretched steering cables, but that was the most exciting part of the race. We were not among the winners.

I did not sail the 1972 SORC but for 1973 I committed myself for the whole Circuit—something I had never done—to sail with George Eddy and Jim Briggs aboard George's new C&C 39, *Windance*. This was to be a family affair as my oldest son "BJ" was engaged by George and Jim to look after *Windance,* keeping her in fighting trim between races, and my wife was to join us for the final week in Miami and Nassau.

Like *Redhead* and *Kittiwake* in the previous races, *Windance* was a new boat. After two short races from Clearwater to Saint Pete and the Venice Race, the Lauderdale Race would be her first test at sea. She proved to be up to the challenge of the stormiest race in the history of the SORC.

The Lauderdale Race that year was light all the way to Rebecca Shoal. With the winds from the south to south-

Saint Petersburg to Fort Lauderdale

east, it was slow going tacking down the Gulf of Mexico, and eerie drifting through large fleets of shrimpers dragging their trawls and brilliantly lighted in the nighttime haze. We stayed well out from the Florida shore, and fetched close to Dry Tortugas on the port tack before taking a final hitch toward Rebecca. As we converged on Rebecca with the fleet it appeared that we were in very good position—most of the boats around us were either larger or among the hottest in our class. We believed we were first among nine C&C 39s.

After passing Rebecca the wind began to pick up from the southeast. Gradually we were forced to change down from the light number-one to the heavy number-one and then to the number-two. Then a reef was in order. Bruce Kirby skippering the Canada's Cup contender, *C-Mirage,* powered through to windward, and aside from this discouraging event—which we seemed unable to do anything about—we were holding our own.

According to the weather forecast we could expect a strong cold front to pass through the area sometime that evening, and the steadily increasing southeast wind tended to confirm that the front was approaching on schedule. After sunset we could see lightning in the distance astern, and gradually the wind came around as we reached up the Florida Keys with the wind over our starboard side.

As we sailed up the Keys we converged with the Stream. By midnight it was rough and increasingly windy. *Windance*'s motion was quick and uncomfortable, and our watch system was threatening to dissolve as most of us had been up off and on all day, and some of us were fighting seasickness. George and BJ were in the cockpit, and I was on the helm when a violent puff heeled us over. *Windance* rounded up, and we broached. This had every sign of being the presager of the cold front; more was to come. We were able to bear away with difficulty, then it happened again.

"Cast off the mainsheet," I shouted to George who was seated next to the sheet winch. *Windance* remained laid over in the wind, her boom end dragging in the water. She wouldn't bear off. Nothing happened, and again I shouted to George to cast off the sheet. It had jammed somehow or George was unable to see how to get at it in the darkness and with the confusion. "I can't get it off, Ted," he hollered back at me, the words barely audible as the wind whipped them off to leeward as he spoke. "Cut the fucking thing," I shouted back to George who appeared suddenly immobilized.

I could "see" the thoughts flashing through George's mind: ". . . my new boat . . . brand new mainsheet . . . cost a lot of money . . . what to do. . . ." There are times when instant action is necessary, drastic measures must be considered and decided in seconds—experience guides you in evaluating all the consequences. Perhaps it was not necessary to cut the mainsheet, but we were pinned on our side by an unrelenting wind. We had to get *Windance* on her feet and under control and then as quickly as possible get the mainsail down. BJ sprang to life from the floor of the cockpit where he had been huddled seeking shelter from the driving rain and the incessant motion. His knife was out and he sliced through the sheet.

Aware of the commotion, Bob Adams appeared from below and, as *Windance* payed off finally and came more nearly upright, he rushed forward to the main halyard and cast it off. BJ went forward to help, and they soon had the sail down and under control. We cast off the topping lift, as there was no sheet to control the boom. George grabbed the boom and held it against the port-side lifeline stanchions until Bob and BJ could come aft and lash it down. This is an approximate account of events which occurred rapidly over about two minutes. I cannot be certain of the details. The essential elements were: broach, cut the mainsheet, lower main, control main boom—all in a screaming wind, heaving seas, and driving rain in the

Saint Petersburg to Fort Lauderdale

pitch black of midnight while steering *Windance* out of the broach.

With the main down, *Windance* hurtled before the wind under the number-two genoa. I had only a general idea of our heading as she would yaw and pitch violently. My main concern was to keep her headed dead downwind to avoid another broach—although she was easier to control under genoa and no mainsail.

Through the rain, ahead and to windward, I saw what appeared to be a large searchlight sweeping back and forth. With the blackness of the night it was impossible to keep one's directional bearings, and with *Windance* swinging wildly through forty or fifty degrees of heading while I struggled to keep her headed before the wind, it was very difficult to tell from one moment to the next where the light would reappear. First it would be abeam, then dead ahead. I was reminded of many times in Long Island Sound when a tug or coastal tanker would approach a fleet of racing sailboats at night. They would play their spotlight back and forth across the horizon trying to pick out the sails of the racing fleet. I surmised that this was what was happening with the light we could see periodically sweeping back and forth. Perhaps a ship had picked up radar echoes from us and other racers near us. I shouted to George to try to keep some sort of bearing on the light to make sure we weren't on a collision course.

It was a fearful night, pitch black except for brilliant flashes of lightning which had now come up on us from astern. The wind was gusting over forty knots, and our speed was hovering around ten. You couldn't see the waves until they came within the circles of light cast by the bow and stern lights, and then it was impossible to react quickly enough to avoid them. Violence was everywhere. The wind, the noise: the rain beat on the hood of my foul-weather gear and hissed in the water alongside. Through it all *Windance* was behaving well, and I had no further difficulty avoiding broaches. Except for the nagging fear that there was a ship out there somewhere nearby, it was an exhilarating ride—the kind that gets the adrenalin flowing and makes you vibrate with life and excitement.

Then the wind *really* blew and with it came a more violent rain that blotted out visibility beyond a tiny circle maybe ten feet in front of our bow and forty feet to either side of the cockpit. *Windance* buried her bow up to the stemhead. The sea hissed—all the spindrift flattened by the driving rain. Lightning crashed all around us, and *Windance* hurtled forward as if pushed by a giant arm. "Where's the light?" I screamed at George—knowing that there was no way he could tell. Even with the compass in front of me I had only a vague idea which direction we were headed. The compass card swung wildly, useless, its magnetic card unable to keep up with our wild movements. My only thought was to keep her dead before the wind. If we were on a collision course with a ship or another yacht there was no way to know, and if we knew, there was no way to do anything differently than what we were doing. We entrusted ourselves to fate.

Pressed down by the wind in the number two, *Windance*'s bow was almost level with the wave tops. Great sheets of water curved back from either side of the bow rising many feet above the deck as they arched aft and outboard. We seemed to be propelled forward in a small area of greenish light—the bow down, the stern lifted as if continuously on the crest of a large wave. With the onslaught of the blast of wind and rain the speedometer needle leaped to the peg at twelve knots, and the anemometer (wind speed) needle spun around to its peg at sixty knots. Both gauges stayed unwavering on their pegs for an indeterminate length of time—thirty seconds? two minutes? five? None of us could be sure, but it was the wildest ride any had experienced—and we numbered among us at least three Transatlantic Races, a couple of dozen Bermuda Races, and countless other ocean races

Saint Petersburg to Fort Lauderdale

and passages. Rock steady in her bow-down attitude, *Windance* flew before the storm.

Eventually the rain diminished slightly. Bob, who was sitting on the starboard cockpit seat alongside BJ, shouted to me, "Shall we take it down?" (meaning the genoa).

"If you think you can," I shouted back, but I didn't want them going forward if they weren't confident that they could hang on and get the sail under control. "We'll get it," BJ said, and they hurried to the bow. In no time the sail was down and furled into the toe rails forward.

The wind seemed to diminish at that very moment. The anemometer needle came off the peg and flung itself wildly between forty and fifty. With no sail set now, *Windance* still flew before the wind at ten knots.

Limited visibility returned, and we were able to determine a course and head approximately on it. We looked around for the light, but it was gone. When Bob came aft, after lowering the genoa, he asked if I wanted relief at the helm. I had felt nothing but excitement and elation during the height of the storm and didn't feel tired now, but I knew that I had been steering a long time and sensed that Bob would like a shot at it. I turned *Windance*'s wheel over to him and collapsed in the cockpit. "Why don't you go below," someone suggested, and I readily agreed—flopping on a bunk below exhausted. I didn't move until we had nearly reached Fort Lauderdale later that day.

We discovered after finishing that we were very likely just beyond a dramatic rescue. In the height of the storm, a seagoing tug towing a barge of molasses took so many seas over her stern that she foundered and eventually sank. Her crew took to a life raft and were rescued by another C&C 39 whose crew saw their distress flares. It seems reasonable that the light we saw was a searchlight from the tug, but we saw no flares and could have seen nothing through the driving rain that enveloped us for so many minutes. It was both a daring and unprecedented rescue under very nearly impossible conditions. Never before had a fleet of ocean-racing sailboats all survived a storm which sank a seagoing ship, and never before had a sailing yacht performed such a rescue.

Later we were to hear that the barge of molasses the tug had been towing drifted ashore on Molasses Reef.

SOMEONE HAS TO BE LAST

Other commitments kept me from racing from Saint Pete to Fort Lauderdale until 1978, and then I was to do it aboard my own boat, *Impertinent,* a custom thirty-footer of my own design. The decision to do the SORC with *Impertinent* wasn't made until December. I had been talking with Walt Levering, a skiing friend from Vermont, about something completely unrelated to sailing. Walt had sailed with us aboard *Kittiwake* in 1965 with his wife Les, and I had seen him briefly in Miami the year before. We commiserated over the phone that neither had plans for the SORC, and when I mentioned I had a boat but no money to campaign it, Walt suggested he could find a crew from Lake Champlain and enough money to pay the expenses of the yacht. And that, in the short version, is how we came to be on the Lauderdale Race in 1978.

Walt, his partner Paul Graves, and I had spent the better part of two weeks preparing *Impertinent* for the Circuit, and we just made it to Saint Pete in time to be inspected and start the Boca Grande Race. Meanwhile, Gibb Smith and Glen Parker had joined us, but the only sailing time we had together was a nighttime trip from the boatyard in Clearwater to the Saint Petersburg Yacht Club. None of the Vermonters had ever sailed on *Impertinent* before, and Walt was the only one of them who had sailed a Circuit.

We finished twelfth in class in the Boca Grande Race

Saint Petersburg to Fort Lauderdale

which, considering our unfamiliarity with the boat and each other was fairly creditable. However, we were unhappy with this result and vowed we could do better in the Lauderdale Race.

Impertinent was one of four half-tonners rating at the bottom of our class (actually, we rated a tenth higher at 21.8). We were the smallest boats in the SORC. Therefore, we expected to see most of the fleet disappear over the horizon and hoped that light conditions would allow us to stay within our time allowance from the larger boats. Two of the half-tonners were new boats and we soon learned that we could not sail competitively with them. Loys Charbonnet's *Checkered Demon* was the same vintage as *Impertinent* (1975) and we seemed to be fairly even with them. Therefore, the prospects for seeing any other yachts after the first day of the Lauderdale Race were dim. If we saw anyone but *Checkered Demon, Hot Flash,* or *Mercury* (the other half-tonners) we would be doing okay.

We were in good position after the start with approximately half of our class behind us when we rounded the fairway buoy leaving Tampa Bay. Most of the fleet headed off slightly west of the rhumb line to Rebecca Shoal.

Our pre-race strategy was to stay east of the rhumb line. The weather forecast predicted light winds during the night shifting to southeast or south the following day. We surmised that the winds would be stronger nearer the Florida coast, that we could hold a faster course during the night and then would be able to lay off for Rebecca when the southeaster came in. Others holding west would, perhaps, have to beat upwind to get to Rebecca. On paper it was a good plan. As the fleet spread out in the haze the first afternoon, we were the only one to hold so far east. If we were right, we would be in fantastic position at Rebecca. If we were wrong . . . ?

Impertinent sailed fast and well all night, and dawn

found us about fifty miles from Rebecca with the wind still forward of the beam on port tack. There wasn't a sail in sight. Visibility was excellent. This was a bit disheartening, but we would wait until we approached Rebecca before passing judgment on our strategy. The wind came around to the southeast as predicted. We were elated. All those to the west would be beating to Rebecca. Then after about two hours, instead of continuing to veer to the south, it came back to east-southeast. Not so good. Still, we maintained cautious optimism.

When Rebecca Shoal hove into sight, there wasn't another thing on the horizon for fifteen miles in any direction. Then we knew: our strategy had failed, we must surely be the last boat to round.

There was nothing to do but forget about our losses and see if we couldn't catch *Checkered Demon* or any of the slower boats in the older boat division. We had found out in the Boca Grande Race that *Impertinent* went particularly well upwind in the rough going, and with the wind now forecast to go right around to the northwest—backing from the southeast with the approach of a cold front—it appeared that we were in for a rough, slogging beat up the Stream.

Our strategy for the beat up the coast to Lauderdale was largely dictated by the weather. The wind came around for us as we passed Rebecca, and we soon found ourselves close-hauled on port tack just barely able to parallel the line of reefs off the Keys. Gradually, where the Keys bend to the north, we approached the Gulf Stream. Soon we were leaping along under number-three genoa and a double-reefed main making six knots through the water and an estimated nine over the bottom. It was rough, but glorious, sailing.

All through the night we slogged to windward on the port tack. It was easy to count our progress to the east as we passed abeam of each of the many lights marking the outlying reef along the Keys. At 1915 I obtained a fix from

Saint Petersburg to Fort Lauderdale

American Shoal and Key West. At 2355 we were abeam of Sombrero Key. At dawn we were off Alligator Reef.

During the daylight hours navigation became much more difficult. Our course, close-hauled, took us away from the Florida coastline and we no longer had visual contact with the reef markers. Our strategy now was to stay in the stream as much as possible to gain maximum benefit from its current. However, this meant that the seas were becoming enormous, kicked up by the northerly wind opposing the current. Navigation below became almost impossible. *Impertinent* lept from wave to wave, and it was all I could do to see the details on the charts. Striking off distances with the dividers was difficult, hazardous (to keep from sticking one's self with the sharp points), and took an unbelievable amount of effort. Walking parallel rulers across the chart was impossible. Eventually I gave up trying to maintain an accurate plot of our positions and settled for an approximate idea. We would tack well before there was any chance of sailing into Bahamian waters and make sure we didn't sail beyond Fort Lauderdale—hardly precise ocean-racing navigation, but close enough to get us there.

There were only two habitable places on board *Impertinent*. If you were below, you wedged yourself into a bunk. If you were on deck, you found a place to sit and something to hang onto. *Impertinent* loved it, thrashing to windward at over six knots, leaping from wave to wave. While I can't honestly say that these were the conditions for which she was designed, I was obviously pleased she handled them so well. But hour after hour of this is extremely taxing. Neither Paul, Glen, nor Gibb had ever seen anything like this, nor had Walt or I ever been in such conditions in so small a boat. I began to wish I had installed handles on the deck so we could reach between our legs and hold ourselves to the deck like a novice rider gripping the saddle horn on a bucking bronco. For food we survived on raisins, candy bars, and Gatoraid. Getting

Saint Petersburg to Fort Lauderdale

anything else out of the galley was impossible.

Late in the afternoon I announced to the crew that I thought a tack to starboard would bring us into the coast somewhere around Key Biscayne. It was entirely possible that I had underestimated the set of the Stream, and I had no desire to overshoot Fort Lauderdale. I didn't even try to use the RDF (we had no Loran aboard) as it would have been impossible to use it below.

The motion across the waves was much easier on the starboard tack. It took us over an hour, and then we saw the Miami skyline. Relieved, I saw that we were, indeed, coming in at Key Biscayne as I had guessed. (Navigators aren't supposed to "guess", they are supposed to "know.")

To our great joy we crossed a relatively large boat and saw another unidentified sail astern of it. Our dreadful slogging had payed off; we had caught some competitors.

Instead of tacking back to port as soon as we were sure of our position, we remained on starboard tack until we were quite close to shore. The motion was so much easier in close out of the current that we couldn't face going back out to the rough water. This was a mistake, of course, but we rationalized that *Impertinent* would be able to sail much faster in the smoother water. There was no way we were going to be able to make up the difference in speed that the faster current offshore would provide. However, it was ever so much more comfortable, and we were all tired, wet, and hungry. We had proven our point. We had caught at least two boats. We were almost home.

It was getting dark as we approached Lauderdale, and the wind had come around more to the west allowing us to ease sheets slightly to make the finish line off the breakwater. Unfortunately, this meant that those who had stayed out in the Stream did not have to take as much of a starboard tack hitch as we had off Miami. The boat that we had crossed in the Stream now moved well ahead, and the boat astern of him was converging on us from offshore. It was *Checkered Demon,* and we cursed our

Saint Petersburg to Fort Lauderdale

chicken hearts that had let him come even with us from hull down astern.

Demon pulled slightly ahead of us as we converged, the boats being within two or three boatlengths of each other. Then strange things began to happen to the wind. With less than two miles to go, the wind stopped completely. Both boats drifted out of control—the slight zephyrs which puffed up occasionally and fitfully were almost impossible to take advantage of with the leftover slop of the seas throwing boat and sails this way and that. At one point *Checkered Demon* was headed straight for us, and we were momentarily concerned that we might collide. Then, ever so perceptibly, we caught a slight puff —*Impertinent* had been headed in the right direction to take advantage of it, *Checkered Demon* had not—and we crept into the lead.

By now we had both drifted close enough to the beach to be concerned. We were maybe four or five waves from the surf, and the wind came back in from the northeast making it a lee shore. Now, instead of an easy reach to the finish, we both had to beat out to the end of the breakwater and the race-committee boat stationed at the finish line. We had no hope of beating *Checkered Demon* on corrected time—our rating was a tenth of a foot higher—but we were determined to beat them boat for boat, just as they were determined to do the same to us if they could.

Suddenly, what had been a dead calm and then the faintest of zephyrs became almost a gale. *Demon* was caught with full-size genoa set (we had up our number-three). Both were faced with short beats to the finish. There was no time to change headsails—and we had pulled out our reefing lines in our haste to set more sail area during the calm. We lugged everything to the finish line—badly overpowered in a wind which was now over thirty knots—and managed to stay ahead of *Checkered Demon* by a couple of minutes.

It was the most exciting finish I've ever had in so long

a race approached only by a similar finish in the '65 Bermuda Race. In both instances we finished next to last and wound up last on corrected time.

It was surely not a glorious finish, but we had sailed a little boat through strenuous conditions. We felt good—especially Paul, Gibb, and Glenn, who had never in their wildest dreams imagined the conditions through which we had just sailed. After hot showers, a hot meal, and steady, warm, dry beds we felt even better.

XII

How It All Started

HAVING GOTTEN THIS FAR, to the final chapter, you will have by now an appreciation for the infinite variability and forever challenging nature of sailing. Then consider that we have really only scratched the surface of one aspect of offshore sailing—small-boat or one-design sailing has been skipped entirely. What a wonderful activity it is. What an incredible affect it has had on my life.

Those of us who have been around a while sometimes forget that we didn't discover the joys of sailing instantly. We take much for granted, even become jaded. It took us years to appreciate our sport fully, and if we remain receptive we rediscover the variety of sailing every time we sail. Young people just being introduced to sailing don't know this automatically. Kids aren't drawn to sailing just because their elders think it's wonderful; in fact, that probably turns them off. Kids have to discover for themselves that sailing is a fun thing to do.

I don't know what turned me on to sailing. I had been exposed to it at an early age, but I don't think anyone in my family made much of a "thing" of it. I remember, when I was very young, becoming engrossed in *Yachting* magazine—sitting on the floor in Art and Louise Utz's living room devouring every page of every issue. Family visits to the Utz house were always special, and I often

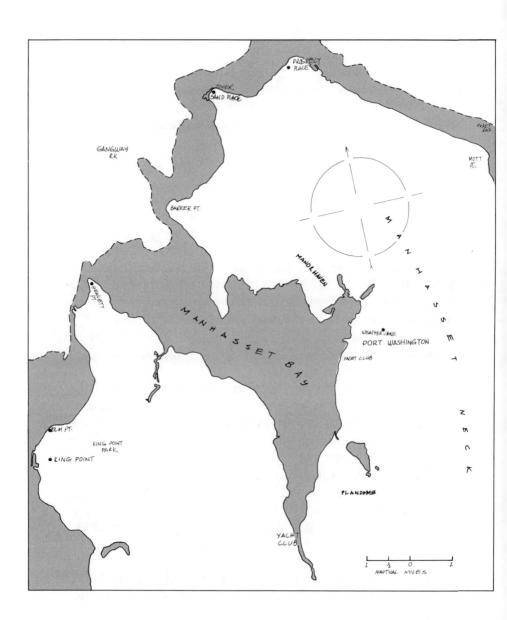

How It All Started

wonder at the coincidence that this house later became the home of Marcia Wiley, *Yachting*'s managing editor. Whatever it was, I missed no opportunity thereafter to learn anything I could about sailing. I didn't care very much for the things I was supposed to read (but Oliver Wendell Holmes's "Old Ironsides" became my anthem). Alfred F. Loomis ("Spun Yarn") and William H. Taylor ("Boatsteerer") who were editors at *Yachting* became my contemporary heroes.

I suppose the fact that I more or less discovered sailing for myself makes me a sucker for youngsters I meet today who take an interest in sailing. I have enjoyed being involved with teaching young people—not only my own children—to sail, and I often wish I could provide them with the kind of experience I had as a junior sailor. Unfortunately, nothing quite like it exists today.

All too often in our formal junior-sailing programs we old fogies tend to forget that sailing isn't always as difficult as we sometimes make it out to be. The basic skills are easily mastered. This, plus sailing's variety, is what makes it a great participant sport. Of course, there are many things that must be mastered beyond the basics, and this adds to sailing's intrigue. Kids can assume and should be given more responsibility than they are often allowed. Young people, when they're learning sailing skills, need to be given the chance to develop them on their own.

Unfortunately, we sometimes get tangled in the warps of our own eagerness to encourage the young to sail and to keep them from getting into trouble. All too often I have seen juniors turn away disenchanted when overzealous race committees canceled races or shortened courses because they thought there was too much wind. Juniors complain that they aren't given good races and committees complain that some of the juniors are irresponsible. Too many programs are nothing more than glorified babysitting services. Kids are pressured into joining, whether or not they have an interest in sailing. In these cases both the unmotivated and the motivated are often turned away from sailing. When they are all dumped into one "boat" it is no wonder that committee chairmen get nervous. On the other hand, when committee chairmen run regattas for the least interested, it is understandable that the highly motivated young people become disenchanted.

Kids know best what is good for kids, and we should listen more to them. In spite of what many parents believe, normal youngsters have strong self-preservation instincts. Given the rudimentary tools of good seamanship which every junior must have before he attends a regatta, the junior will probably behave with more prudence than would many adults. Invariably they have a better feel for the limits of safety than someone sitting on a dock or aboard a committee boat.

In my junior days I enjoyed an experience which, I think, perfectly illustrates this point. The Meteor Class Sailboat Association, of which I was a member for only five years of its forty-year history, was not a brief accident but a continuing demonstration of the good judgment of everyday, run-of-the-mill kids.

The Meteor was designed in 1927 by Charles D. Mower. It was set up as a junior boat with an association of juniors and given a strong, well-thought-out constitution and bylaws. The boat was sixteen feet overall, vee-bottomed, weighed around four hundred pounds—which wasn't bad for a cedar-on-oak hull—and carried 154 square feet of sail, only 25 of which was in the jib. In retrospect, the only thing the Meteor lacked was a spinnaker, and if she had one they might be racing still. Meteors were spirited performers for their day; only forty-six were built, but they raced actively every year from 1927 into the 1960s.

It wasn't the boat that made the Meteor Class a success—although the spritely performance surely helped.

How It All Started

The Meteor Class was for kids and *they* ran it. Youngsters from about thirteen to eighteen raced their boats and ran the races. They lived by their constitution and bylaws, making amendments when, in their judgment, they were necessary. They defended the boat rules like a religion and ran class affairs with a responsible conservatism that I find quite remarkable on reflection.

Adult supervision of the Meteor Class was nonexistent, although adult interest and encouragement was usually present and welcome. The kids always had help when they asked for it, but they never had unwanted interference. The sailing instructor was the "head man" (although often a girl), and was invariably one of the better and/or more popular immediate graduates (too old to race) whom the kids elected. Thus the class was perpetuated over the years. The oldest person directly involved was nineteen or twenty and served at the pleasure of his or her peers. That's how it evolved, generation after generation.

When I was a member we'd race Monday, Wednesday, and Friday afternoons. Those of us who were eager sailed or worked on our boats the other days. Occasionally a parent would race on weekends. We never missed a race because someone told us it was too rough to go out or for any other reason that we didn't originate ourselves. If the wind was up, we'd have an informal meeting on the dock and take a vote (the instructor's experience carried considerable authority). If the majority wanted to race most of us would. No one ridiculed those who didn't go. No one was a "sissy" who opted out. If the majority didn't want to race nobody went. Sure, there would be occasional grumbling from the minority, but if we voted not to race we'd stage water fights or do something else inappropriate instead.

The Meteor Class not only taught us how to handle our boats under a variety of conditions, but it taught us how to handle ourselves. We learned self-sufficiency

How It All Started

afloat and self-reliance in many realms. We did all the kooky things kids have always done. We sometimes gave our parents gray hairs, but what kids have not. None of us drowned or ever came close to having a serious accident; while a few of our less fortunate contemporaries killed themselves in automobiles.

I was fourteen my first year in the Meteors. I used a borrowed boat which belonged to the "graduating" sailing instructor whose family wanted to save the boat for his still too young little sister. It had no name, it was just "Number 32" which at that time was the newest boat in the class—and probably the fastest. Later I owned two Meteors, one of which I had built.

My first race was incredible. The course was from the Port Washington Yacht Club dock to "three-can" (Can number-three in the harbor channel), to a mooring buoy on the edge of the PWYC anchorage, to the dock. It was a reach all the way around in a light easterly wind. Soon after the start, my crew—Dick Higgins—and I found ourselves in first place. I hadn't the vaguest idea how we got there, and even less idea how to stay there. What a terrible responsibility to be leading when you don't know anything about racing. Naturally Dick and I did not discuss these thoughts, although I'm sure his were similar to mine. It was desperation that kept us in the lead. We concentrated as hard as we could, trying to emulate what those close astern were doing to try to pass us. We not only held our lead to three-can, to our utter amazement we increased it. (We were too dumb to know that on a close reach the lead boat has a large advantage provided by the laws of aerodynamics.)

It was a long broad reach to the mooring buoy, and Judy Sutherland—who was an "old hand" of seventeen favored to win the season championships (she did)—began to catch up. Judy moved slightly ahead by the time we approached the mooring buoy, and if I had known my racing rules I could have forced her to make room for us

How It All Started

to round the mark inside. Had I done so, we would have retained the lead, but I let her get in, circled around, and rounded behind her—following her to the finish line.

Reflecting on those early days I am surprised how much we didn't know about racing sailboats—the things we never learned in four years of sailing. This is the price we paid for being insular, sailing only among ourselves because there were no other Meteor fleets. Today's kids get around more and learn more from being beaten by hotshots outside their own mud puddle. We did learn good seamanship, though. We also learned to practice good judgment, and we had a lot of fun which reinforced the lessons. Dick and I were so engrossed with the fun we were having learning to race that first summer that we didn't realized how well we were doing. The first realization that we finished second for the season was upon seeing my name engraved on the trophy at our awards party. What a thrill!

Above all other considerations we had fun in the Meteors. What about *safety?* Safety was part of the fun. If we felt scared or unsafe we weren't having fun. Of course we did some foolish things, but our innate cautiousness kept us from going over our heads. Our small mistakes snapped us back quickly and taught us respect for the water. Through our association with the Meteors we acquired a firm base for an activity that could give us pleasurable diversion and a way of life. We used to be derisive of the club sailing classes which were typical of the programs offered today. It's no wonder we felt superior to the adult-controlled "sailing kindergartens" when we had total control of our own class.

The Meteor Class was a rare thing, a unique experience. It was the kind of experience I would like to see all kids have but few can get now. It was the beginning of something for me, and I cannot help but wonder if any of the experiences recounted in the previous chapters would have happened had I not received the special introduction to sailing afforded by the Meteor Class Sailboat Association.

A few years ago I caught sight of a familiar object while driving under the I-95 Bridge over the Mianus River in Connecticut. I stopped to examine the disreputable pile of boards which had once been a boat. There was no question, it was a Meteor, I still remembered every line, every plank and frame of that boat. I could almost tell what its number had been (at least I could tell some that it was not). I considered trying to locate the owner and offering to buy it—without a lot of work it would never sail again—but I did not.

Am I'm sorry I didn't? I'm not sure.